# *Tales From the JanVan*

## Lessons on Life & Camping

# Tales From
# the JanVan

## Lessons on Life & Camping

Jan Stafford Kellis

Myrno Moss Perspectives

## Also By Jan Stafford Kellis

### Fiction:

*The Word That You Heard*
*Superior Sacrifices*
*The Sunshine Room*

### Nonfiction:

*Bookworms Anonymous, Volumes I and II*
*A Pocketful Of Light*
*Bookworms Anonymous Cookbooklet*

For all of the women who want to travel.
Go forth and wander free.

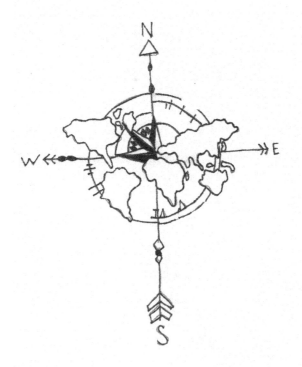

A good traveler has no fixed plans and is not
intent on arriving.

*- Lao Tzu -*

# ITINERARY

# ORIGINAL MAP

Road Trip Rule # 7:

No plan is final.

# On-Ramp

I always thought that if my life fell apart it would be caused by one dramatic event. A cataclysmic trauma capable of derailing my carefully planned trajectory and depositing me in a dark and dirty ditch, defeated and forlorn, forever changed. There would be a clearly defined before and after—like crossing a border.

I thought this way because I'd witnessed the derailment of others' lives and listened to their stories of befores and afters. They could pinpoint a tidy, transformative event—meeting their mate, accepting a job, or dropping out of college—that split their life stories into two distinct chapters. A neat bifurcation.

But I've learned that a life can derail in stages.

For me, the derailing began in November 2015 when my husband Jason asked for a divorce after fifteen years of marriage. Losing the person I'd thought I'd never lose felt like a sinkhole opening in the center of my chest. The loss whisked me into a long, dark tunnel with no light at the end.

At first, I stubbornly pretended I'd planned to enter this tunnel. I focused on buying and renovating a house and spent my days chatting with contractors and painting walls and selecting new furniture. Each night, I fell into bed (my nephew's lower bunk) exhausted, too tired to wonder how or when I would exit the darkness.

Meanwhile, my body knew the truth and built roadblocks to progress: my appetite vanished and hives covered my torso like tire tracks of trauma.

Eventually, the house was transformed, the hives disappeared, and I felt semi-functional. I wasn't yet sure where the road was headed, but at least I was on it.

The following summer, another derailment. My mom died in a completely unexpected way and five months later, both of my daughters were living 3000 miles from home.

Fate didn't apologize, didn't help me navigate back to the safe streets. She had her driving gloves on and left the road map at home. After a while, I learned to regard Fate's assaults as traffic signals, a chance to pause and decide where to go next. It turns out there is no traffic cop for life. Nobody blows the whistle when you make a questionable choice; nobody tells you when to proceed, when to turn left, when to stay the course.

When I finally realized nobody is directing me and learned to relish the freedom and chaos of directing myself, real life began. The crazy wonderful wild life that can only happen because of past choices: All of the broken promises, the poor decisions, the fantastical dreams and brief jolts of pure happiness delivered me here, to this crossroads upon which I'm poised to choose my next right path.

My Class B motorhome—the Jan Van—became the vehicle (literally) that carried me through the tunnel of grief and out the other side.

This is the story of how I re-mapped my life and of some of the adventures I had along the way.

Sit back and enjoy the ride.

Road Trip Rule # 13:

Every trip begins with an idea.

## The Rolls K'Nardly

Travel is my drug of choice. It's more potent than caffeine and as addictive as heroin. It's mood-altering, unfiltered, legal, and doesn't require a prescription. It's socially acceptable, non-fattening, non-allergenic, and non-hallucinogenic (except during road trips after 36 hours of driving).

Fortunately, it's also habit-forming.

If there is a travel gene, I have it. I was born traveling—Mom was three months along when Dad, a geophysicist, accepted a job prospecting for nickel in Australia. Much of the time, Dad had to live "out bush" in a primitive camp comprised of corrugated tin buildings and an outhouse or two. Mom sometimes joined him as the camp cook.

They took a short break for my birth before returning to the outback. We lived at various exploration camps for most of my first two years, a time well-documented in Mom's letters home and the large, unruly collection of photographic slides that now resides in my basement. The photos present a study of flat ochre earth, sparse brush, and my infant self bathing in a tin tub in the middle of the red dirt yard. There are shots of kangaroos, emus, koalas, and of Dad riding his motorcycle, bush hat firmly planted on his head. One photo shows a carefully composed portrait of a Huntsman spider the size of an apple pie. We returned to Michigan before my third birthday. I have no conscious memory of those early travels, but I grant them partial credit for my lifelong wanderlust.

I've racked up my fair portion of airline miles, but my favorite way to travel is the iconic American road trip in my class B motorhome to a long-dreamed-of destination. I control the schedule, the timing, and where and when I'll stop and view the vistas.

My love of road travel ramped up in the 1970s

when my dad purchased a fifteen-year-old US Air Force van the shape and size of a UPS truck and converted it into a motorhome.

He painted the navy exterior a blinding silver so it would reflect the heat rather than attract it, as the original hue had done. Next, he insulated and carpeted the interior (floors, walls, and ceiling) in green Berber and built a dinette in the back that converted into bunkbeds to accommodate the four of us—Mom and Dad on the bottom, my sister Jen (still a toddler) on the top bunk next to me. He built a kitchen counter with a sink and added cubbies everywhere. Finally, he installed a refrigerator and a composting toilet and added a bench seat covered in fake arctic fox fur near the front of the van behind the engine.

The engine was nestled inside a metal trapezoidal cabinet next to the driver's seat, just below the billboard-sized windshield. It lacked the power required to propel the van at highway speed. An eight-cylinder engine simply wouldn't fit into the space, so Dad replaced the straight six engine with a V-6. I didn't understand the challenge or benefit of replacing the engine, but this part of the project was Dad's favorite dinner party topic for months. I can still recall him describing the tripod and pulley system he fashioned to lift the old engine out and lower the new one in, and his self-congratulatory smile when he described the incremental increase in power the new engine provided. Only after our guests emitted oohs and aahs would the conversation travel to more interesting territory.

I remember the day Dad named the rig. We were cooking along at our top speed of 55 mph on a sunny April morning in 1979, threading our way west along US-2 toward the Black Hills of South Dakota when Dad said, "Let's call this thing the Rolls K'Nardly."

Mom and I must have looked at him askance, waiting for an explanation or a punchline.

His grin promised a punchline.

"It rolls downhill," he paused, "and it k'nardly roll uphill."

The Rolls K'Nardly it was. Dad even made a bumpersticker, which turned out to be a great campground conversation starter when people strolled past our campsite in the evenings and asked about the name tag on our homemade motorhome.

We must've traveled a million miles in that van. We took family trips to New Mexico, Texas, and South Dakota, all from our home in the eastern end of Michigan's Upper Peninsula (the UP). We traveled to Wisconsin, Minnesota, and circled Lake Superior. Several times per year, Mom drove Jen and me across the UP to visit Grandma and Great Grandma in the Copper Country. We even took the Rolls K'Nardly to the drive-in theatre to see the original Star Wars movie, smug in our ability to cook and eat dinner while we watched the show, unconcerned whether we blocked the view for others.

There was no standard heater in the van. A black

tube diverted heat from the engine to a wide hole above the front passenger-side wheel well and blasted hot air directly at the front bench seat. We jammed a cube of foam rubber the size of my head into the heater hole to reduce the risk of heat stroke during summer trips.

Of course, there was no air conditioning. The two front doors slid back to open, and one tiny window on the driver's side was the only one that allowed air to enter. Dad installed a ceiling vent to provide slight relief from the heat.

The undersized engine, unrelenting heat, and lack of air conditioning weren't the only quirks we tolerated. The Rolls K'Nardly also burned through a fan belt every 500 miles or so. Sometimes a preemptory squeal would alert us, sometimes the idiot light on the dashboard was the first sign of trouble. The van would suddenly lose power and we'd coast to a stop.

Dad bought a case of fan belts each spring, and when I turned nine, he determined I was old enough to replace them while he watched.

The routine ran thus: the driver parked on the shoulder of the highway and cranked the steering wheel as far right as it would go. We'd allow fifteen minutes or so for the engine to cool off while I changed into my fan belt maintenance outfit (perpetually dirty) and prepared for the required bodily contortions by cracking my knuckles and rotating my shoulders.

I'd scootch backwards behind the front driver's side tire until I could no longer see Dad's feet. I made no sudden moves under there since my first lesson when a rookie hair toss had greased and scraped my cheekbone. Any nose itches or errant hairs would have to wait until I emerged. From this position I could snake one hand up into the van's gizzard and pull out the old belt if it hadn't already landed on the road. I'd then install the new one, carefully hooking it around the uppermost wheel before stretching it around the lower one. Dad supervised my work. He would crouch down and hunch over, reluctant to touch the ground with anything but the toes of his shoes, and peer up into the dim engine cavity.

"Good job," he'd pronounce, and I'd inhale his praise and hold it in as long as I could. I'd shimmy out from beneath, back into the daylight and away from the odor of hot engine grease. I'd wash my hands and arms and change back into my regular clothes for the next 500 miles, and then we'd do it all again.

There were no seat belts in the Rolls K'Nardly. Mom sat on the passenger bench and wrapped her arms around Jen straitjacket-style to thwart her escape attempts—sometimes it seemed like Jen had eight limbs—and we spent many miles playing games and singing songs, all uttered in whispers so as not to disturb Dad while he drove. Dad was the kind of traveler who remained jovial as long as nothing went awry, and we acted accordingly.

My job was Chief Navigator. Dad would give me a general direction, such as "aim us toward Tulsa" and I'd open the tattered, spiral-bound Rand McNally atlas and compare our location with the new target. The Rolls K'Nardly was the road-trip equivalent of the embarrassing uncle at a family reunion, and its top speed matched that of a regal procession, so we avoided Interstates. I'd call out directions as we rolled onward, encountering each town named on the map. Even then, I found it supremely satisfying to view each place through the windshield as we cruised through it. Like the sidewalk painting Mary Poppins stepped into, the lines and titles from the paper map grew into a three-dimensional reality before my eyes. Navigating felt like a large-scale scavenger hunt, each town a clue confirming we were moving in the right direction.

I have my own RV now and it doesn't eat fan belts like light afternoon snacks. It can cruise at a respectable speed on the Interstate and it has air conditioning, a separate bedroom, an onboard generator, and a roomy shower. Oh, and there's no fake fur.

I've traveled thousands of miles in it already, navigating by atlas and GPS, all over Michigan and Wisconsin, throughout New England, Prince Edward Island, the Blue Ridge Mountains, and as far west as Kansas City. It's a stylish ride, but it lacks a certain character.

Sometimes I feel the ghosts of my parents riding

shotgun, watching the world blur past, and for a moment I miss the Rolls K'Nardly and its trail of fan belt crumbs.

## Running Away

We sold the Rolls K'Nardly in the mid-80s, and our habit of road-tripping screeched to a halt. My parents replaced traveling with hosting foreign exchange students—instead of visiting the world, we invited the world into our home. We hosted a different student from a different country each year for five years when I was in my early teens. The exchange students used the bedroom that adjoined mine—you had to walk through mine to get to hers—and as soon as I got used to one foreign "sister" traipsing through, she would leave and the next one would arrive. We squired them around to nearby sights—Tahquamenon Falls, Mackinac Island, Castle Rock—but rarely left the state.

Looking back now, I don't know what kindled the interest in becoming a host family for foreign students. It was Dad's decision—our lives were governed by his interests and expectations—and Mom supported it, as she did most of his whims. They became area representatives for the exchange company, which entailed helping other families in the eastern UP connect with students and organizing soirees for the students and families within their territory.

Quite a few non-camping years slid by. Dad and I stopped speaking to each other at some point, for all of the typical reasons: unobserved curfews, inappropriate boyfriends, hormonal mayhem. He wanted me to inch toward adulthood at parade speed; I longed for a drag race.

The first time I ran away from home I was seventeen years old. On the last day of my junior year in high school, I finished my exams and drove away. My getaway car was a banana yellow Ford Pinto Wagon with four on the floor that guzzled oil and sipped gas. The rearview mirror worked, but I didn't bother glancing into it.

I ran to prove my dad wrong about my boyfriend

Ed; I knew the route I'd chosen was a one-way street and I'd never be welcomed back. Dad legally emancipated me within weeks of my departure. We didn't speak for the next nineteen years.

A year after my exit, Dad followed my lead. He returned to school to become an RN, eventually moving out west to work in a VA Hospital.

Ed and I moved to Sault Ste. Marie, an hour's drive from my childhood home. Shortly thereafter, I was caught in the roundabout of young motherhood with two daughters, marriage, and career. Travel became a distant memory.

Ed and I split when I was in my late twenties, and a year later I met Jason.

It felt like coming home. We clicked immediately, and it seemed like everything I'd done up to that point was designed to merge my path with his. He married all of us: my daughter Dani was a bridesmaid and her sister Steph was our flower girl. For the first time in conscious memory, I felt truly happy.

We both loved to camp. We started with a tent and quickly added a blow-up mattress. One morning we woke up at the tail end of a rainstorm—everything was soaked through—and we knew it was time to buy a camper. We purchased an old pop-up camper, then exchanged it for a pull-behind camper with bunk beds for the girls a few years later. Eventually we upgraded to a larger pull-behind camper with a slide-out. We camped with groups of friends, we camped alone, we camped our way from Michigan to Florida and back again.

Jason shared my retirement dream to drive a small motorhome around the United States and Canada at whim, returning home when we felt like it, and hitting the road for extended periods whenever our moods changed. With Jason, my life had a clear trajectory. We'd attained empty-nest status, and we were within ten years of retirement. I envisioned a simple map: a dotted line meandering from Point A to Point B.

I could see our future together as if viewing it through a camper window at night: the cozy glow of candlelight, the two of us sitting close on the couch, a grandchild or two playing on the rug. Safety and security, comfort and joy.

But after fifteen years of marriage, Jason asked for a divorce. I found myself living alone for the very first time. I was forty-five and my daughters were grown and living on their own. In a way, I was living backwards: living without responsibilities felt like my second shot at a carefree young adulthood. The advantages of being a forty-something woman in a twenty-something life included more money and (hopefully) less folly. I finally knew what I liked, and what I wanted to do.

I wanted to travel.

By this time, I'd been working at the local electric utility for nearly twenty years, and my job featured flex time as one of its benefits. My habit was to work four ten-hour days each week and take three days off out of every seven. I considered myself three-sevenths retired.

Now when I try to forecast my future it looks like a recently shaken snow globe. There are some vague shapes, but I can't tell what they are. My map has a Point A, and there are an infinite number of potential Point Bs. I don't know which one I'll visit first

I'd envisioned living out this dream with Jason, but it was time to abandon that notion and make things happen for myself.

For now, I could do this three days per week and during my paid vacation time, which was six weeks per year.

I could test drive retirement.

I could run away on a whim.

I could choose my next Point B.

I just needed the motorhome. In my mind, I'd already begun to call it the Jan Van.

# COMPASS BEARINGS

Road Trip Rule # 17:

Live to camp. Camp to live.

## Camping, Defined

Camping is generally defined as a recreational activity that includes spending at least one night in temporary accommodations in a rural area. The temporary accommodations might be a lean-to made of lashed-together boughs, a sleeping bag beneath the stars, a tent, travel trailer, motorhome, or any other shelter. Humans started camping shortly after they started building homes in which to live, and from which they desired a brief escape.

The man generally haled as the founder of modern camping was Thomas Hiram Holding. An Englishman who discovered his love for camping during a vacation to America, Holding slept on the banks of the Mississippi River for five weeks in the 1850s. He explored parts of the Rocky Mountains on a wagon train before returning to England, where he became a tailor and camped on weekends. Holding spent a few weeks in Ireland on a bicycling/camping trip, which he wrote about in his 1898 book *Cycle and Camp in Connemara*. In 1908, he wrote *The Camper's Handbook*, the first-ever guide to recreational camping.

In the US, people fabricated RVs for their own use shortly after Ford started rolling Model Ts off the assembly line. The new way to camp—hauling a fully-assembled shelter on wheels rather than stowing a folded canvas tent in the cargo area—caught on fast.

The January-February 1936 issue of Trailer Travel Magazine featured an article by noted economist and analyst Roger W. Babson entitled, "We'll Soon Be Living on Wheels". He cited rising property taxes, house maintenance costs, and unpleasant neighbors as reasons Americans were choosing to leave their "immobile homes" and strike out on the road. He identified salesmen and recent retirees as the largest subgroup within the increasing mobile population and predicted that within twenty years of his writing the article, "more than half the population of the United States will be living in automobile trailers".

Heather Long's November 12, 2018 article in the Washington Post proved Babson's prediction wrong by stating that one million Americans, or less than three percent, live in their RVs full-time. These "modern nomads" seem to agree it's cheaper to live in an RV than in a traditional house, but the most common reason cited for choosing a mobile lifestyle is the ability to change the scenery at whim. Quite a few Millennials (those born 1983-2000) are becoming "digital nomads", modern minimalists living on the road and using a laptop and a WiFi connection to maintain their full-time jobs or run their businesses.

Today, there are all types of campers, from purists who sleep in tents they pitch themselves (or in a sleeping bag under the stars) to those who pilot luxury RVs to plush resorts. Some refer to the luxury RV campers as "glampers", short for glamorous campers. This is pronounced with a condescending eye roll and a jealous bite.

I don't care what it's called. I just want to bring my house on vacation.

Road Trip Rule # 29:

There's no such thing
as a wrong turn.

## Later Than You Think

The first thing I noticed when I walked into my friend Sandy's newly renovated kitchen was the whimsical cerulean blue lettering on the far wall. *Enjoy yourself! It's later than you think.*

The phrase was meant to remind Sandy and her guests to revel in the present moment, but it left me vaguely unsettled. I've often recalled the words with a powerless sense of time whooshing past at the speed of an Olympic bobsled.

My recent divorce was still so fresh I couldn't bring myself to utter the word, and I felt disoriented and unmoored. Navigating through each day became a monolithic task. My previously neat and tidy life seemed like a dream in which Jason and I had traveled a scenic road side by side, in no hurry to reach the horizon. His plea for a return to singlehood left me feeling abandoned, facing a rusted out sign full of bullet holes that read: Bridge Out. Road Closed.

We sold our tow-behind camper and split the money. I deposited my half into my Jan Van fund.

*It's later than you think,* I thought. *Start shopping now.*

My search for an RV began with tentative, sporadic internet searches. Whenever I had a free moment I'd find myself scrolling the seemingly endless inventory of dealers within 500 miles of my home address. My memories of our trips in the Rolls K'Nardly assumed a rosy glow. Those were grand adventures, and I wanted to create my own version of them (hopefully, without the fan belt replacements). I wasn't yet sure what I wanted to buy—I figured I'd know it when I saw it. I had $20,000 to spend, which seemed unrealistic at best. I told myself part of the challenge was to find something affordable, and I approached it with the zeal of a nine-year-old on a scavenger hunt.

In June of 2016, my sister Jen and I had lunch with Mom. As usual, we were at Jen's, since she had the largest kitchen. We took turns chopping and stirring while we talked. The three of us had always been close—we had the matching coffee cups, matching kitchen gadgets, and matching blue eyes to prove it.

While we ate, the three of us discussed Mom's upcoming trip to our family cabin in the Keweenaw, a six-hour drive from home. My great-great grandfather, John Paul Petermann, had purchased the property in the late 1800s. He'd managed the Eagle River Hotel there until a fire consumed all but the employees' bunkhouses. Instead of rebuilding the hotel, John Paul decided to use the property as a private family camp, and he temporarily joined the bunkhouses together. It still stands today, a Dr. Seuss-style cabin with tilting floors and a swaybacked roof. The property is now owned by my cousin Chris.

"The River" was Mom's favorite summer destination. She'd spent many childhood summers there and enjoyed recreating some of her favorite memories by swimming in Lake Superior and watching the sunset and visiting friends. When we were kids, we frequently stayed at The River and visited my grandmother and great grandmother, who both lived nearby. The cabin was rich in nooks and crannies; shelves and ledges of all sizes displayed our collected rocks in Mason jars and our library of decades-old Woman's Day and National Geographic magazines, ready to re-read each summer. There were no bare walls. My Aunt Karen had painted murals on the walls of the kitchen and dining room, and my

Grandma Jean had tacked up photographs of wild animals with yellowing bits of cellophane tape.

We had different rules at the cabin. Watching the sunset was required and non-negotiable. Greeting Lake Superior upon arrival, and bidding her farewell upon departure, was expected. We could wear our shoes in the house. We could sleep in one of the bedrooms or outside in a tent. Cinnamon toast was a given, as was thimbleberry jam. We were never, ever, ever, under any circumstances, allowed to swim in Eagle River or venture past the mowed area of the yard. The river hid a murderous undertow, and poison ivy lurked in the tall grass.

Mom shared her plans about which friends she was meeting and where they would dine.

"I'm an old lady," she said. "We like to think about where we're going to eat." She was 72.

"Women in our family live to be nearly a hundred," I said.

"We'll let you know when you can start calling yourself old," said Jen.

We didn't realize this was our last lunch as a trio. Most of her life, Mom was healthy and strong. She gardened, skied, hiked, snowshoed, and canoed. She also enjoyed reading, sewing, embroidery, and cooking. She spent her summers barefoot and knew how to swim. I mean, *really* swim. She'd been on her high school swim team and was fluent in at least twelve different strokes, which she announced as she performed them. "Scissor kick!" She'd yell out.

"Australian crawl!" I lost interest in swimming after mastering the dog paddle.

My mother wasn't your average superhero—she was the kind of superhero who might glance up from the book she was reading, calmly curtail an apocalypse, and return her gaze to the page; the kind, I'd subconsciously convinced myself, who would thwart death.

She had earned her Bachelor's Degree in Chemistry from Michigan Technological University, and returned to school in her forties to receive a teaching degree from Northern Michigan University. After retiring from her teaching position in St. Ignace and her part-time position in the lab at the water department in DeTour, she was diagnosed with rheumatoid arthritis. By then, she was sixty-five and struggling to adjust to life without the structure of a professional schedule. She had both hips replaced and used a cane, though she treated it more like an accessory than a support device. She dangled it from one wrist while she walked and often left it behind when she visited someone. It frequently clattered to the floor when she leaned it on the table during our luncheons.

We weren't worried about her solo journey to the cabin. She loved to drive across the UP, including the eye-glazing half-hour slog through the swamp known as the Seney Stretch. She'd planned to arrive at the cabin on Sunday and head home ten days later to attend my library presentation for my newest book,

*The Sunshine Room.*

Nine days after our luncheon, I was at work when my phone buzzed. I was surprised to see my cousin Chris's name pop up on my caller ID. We are the kind of cousins who rarely contact each other, but when we do, it's as if we've never been apart. My doom meter must've shorted out that day—it never crossed my mind that he was calling with bad news.

"Hello, cousin!"

"Jan. You might want to sit down."

Still, I had no sense of alarm. Chris was sarcasm personified. He delivered every wry observation with a lift of one eyebrow and a deadpan tone.

I laughed. "I *am* sitting down. I'm in my work truck, but I'm parked. What's up?"

"I have bad news."

This was the moment I started listening. Had something happened to his mother, my Aunt Karen? Or to one of his brothers? Or one of our other uncles or aunts? And why was he the one calling? My mom was the official family messenger—the bearer of all news, good and bad.

"The Eagle River Sheriff called me a few minutes ago." He spoke in an even monotone. "The next door neighbors called the Sheriff this morning when your mom didn't answer the door."

The world narrowed to a pinpoint. My entire body went numb. I watched my hands pull my Bullet Journal out of my purse and transcribe the conversation. This was too big to grasp and I knew

I'd need to refer to my notes later. My hands shook as I operated the pen, which left a nearly illegible scrawl across the page.

I thought about how small Mom had looked in the hospital bed during her hip replacement surgeries, and how much she hated the role of patient. I hoped her hips were alright and she hadn't somehow sustained an injury that would require more surgery.

Chris took a couple of breaths while I stared out the windshield. I worried that I'd gone deaf and missed something, but then he spoke again. "She fell down last night in the dining room. The medical examiner said her femur had broken and ripped her femoral artery."

An eternal beat of silence.

"Wait, medical examiner?"

"She was already gone when the sheriff found her. The neighbor identified her. I'm sorry." One tiny part of my brain realized this was probably the most difficult phone call he'd ever made.

If there's such a thing as stress-induced laryngitis, I have it. It locks up my voice during emotionally wrought situations, leaving me with a whisper as dry and fragile as a dead leaf.

"But, are they sure?" I croaked.

"I have the phone number for the medical examiner. Would you like to talk to him directly?"

I jotted down the phone numbers for the medical examiner and the sheriff.

"Thank you for calling," I whispered.

"I didn't want you to hear this from anyone else," he said. "And I've already told my mom, and she's alerting the rest of the family in Alaska except Dani. We figured you'd want to tell her and Steph yourself."

"Okay. I'll call Jen, then the kids."

"Keep me in the loop."

We said our good-byes and ended the call.

I called my sister, whose incredulity matched my own. "Call the medical examiner," she said. "There must have been a mistake."

The medical examiner picked up on the fourth ring.

"People say they fell and broke their femur," he said. He sounded old and weak, pushing his voice as if it had to travel uphill through the phone lines. "But the femur breaks first, causing the fall. Your mom wouldn't have suffered. The rapid blood loss caused her to lose consciousness before she would've realized what had happened. I've seen this before."

I knew he meant this information to comfort me but my mind's eye provided a heart-wrenching vision of Mom all alone, lying on the cold, slanted floor of the dining room staring at the chair legs while she breathed her last few breaths.

Mom had always been the strong one—she'd referred to herself as 'disgustingly robust'—and before her rheumatoid arthritis diagnosis, she'd rarely succumbed even to a common cold. I found her lying on the couch twice during the seventeen years I lived with her, both times for less than an hour. She never suffered headaches, backaches, or stomach aches, unlike my dad, who carried a miniature pharmacy in his pockets to address his chronic manifold maladies.

The day before Mom died, one of my former co-workers passed away. He'd been retired for several years and was one month younger than Mom. Six weeks later, two more friends succumbed—one of them only fifty, and in good shape. She had a pulmonary embolism. And about two months after Mom passed, my good friend Delores died. She was 82 and living in long term care, so her death wasn't as unexpected as the others, but I'd reached my limit. I walked through the church at Delores's wake, clutching her son's arm, before exiting through the side door to vomit in the bushes and have a full, public breakdown on the sidewalk.

The funerals kick-started an invisible, relentlessly ticking clock. The sound was deafening. It was my own Tell-Tale Heart, cautioning me to stop dilly dallying and make my travel dreams happen.

I was forty-six years old with no time to waste.

I could hear the Rolls K'Nardly whisper, "*Enjoy yourself. It's later than you think.*"

Road Trip Rule # 33:

Embrace your inner tourist.
Tour anything and everything.

## Wayside Ahead:
## Bullet Journals

I'm a reformed planner junkie. I've tried every planner, agenda, and calendar available on the free market. None of them were quite right—not the stapled ones, not the bound ones, not the ring binders. The squares were too large, or too small, or the weekly spread was too wide, or too narrow, or the daily spreads had way too much room on some days and not nearly enough on others.

I lost sleep over the Planner Conundrum.

I made my own planner a few times, but what worked for the first few weeks didn't work so well when spring break arrived, or when summer hit, or when I was too busy or not busy enough.

In 2013, I discovered the Bullet Journal, and all of my planner problems were solved. It's so simple, I can't believe I didn't think of it myself. The Bullet Journal was originally developed by Ryder Carroll, a young man diagnosed with ADHD. He devised this method to keep track of everything and relieve his brain of myriad details he'd been attempting to track and remember. He has a video on YouTube, which you can find by searching for his name, that succinctly demonstrates his Bullet Journal method.

The beauty of the Bullet Journal is that it's customizable to every person, for every day or only on the days it's needed. There are a million different ways to set up and use a Bullet Journal, and none of them are wrong.

Traditional Bullet Journals have an index in the front, a monthly spread for each month, and trackers for various habits or practices, such as drinking water or exercising. Writers might set up a tracker to keep track of their writing, to ensure they're producing a specific number of words each day and/or ensure they're keeping their daily writing habit resolution. Most Bullet Journals also feature To-Do Lists and other notes about anything life requires us to manage or maintain. There are certain key symbols Ryder Carroll uses to indicate what type of item each entry is—for example, an event, a task, an idea, or something that requires some other action—but of course you can customize your own journal however you'd like.

If you plug the phrase "bullet journal" into Google or Pinterest, you'll find thousands of examples, many of which feature professional-level artistic doodles. Don't be discouraged by the high-level art you'll find on the Internet—my Bullet Journal has a rather pedestrian appearance, but it's highly efficient.

Your Bullet Journal will become the book you carry everywhere. You'll grab it when you receive a phone call from the insurance company or tax preparer, when you're asked to organize an event, when you're ready to plan your next vacation, or when your cousin calls with devastating news. It's a great place to jot down a recipe someone shared with you, or the one you modified, in case you ever want to make it again. Your Bullet Journal will quickly become the most valuable book you own—an irreplaceable record of your current life, lifestyle, projects, ideas, goals, and plans.

My favorite notebook to use for a Bullet Journal has a name I can't pronounce: the Leuchtturm 1917, which can be found in several colors on Amazon.com. I buy the one with dot grid pages, but they make several different patterns. The Leuchtturm 1917 has pre-numbered pages, which is useful when populating the index list in the front of the book, and it has a sturdy envelope inside the back cover. You can purchase a pen loop that fits it perfectly, and you can add page tabs to mark each monthly spread and other important entries.

If you're not yet ready to invest $20-$25 in a notebook and pen for this purpose, grab a plain notebook and start your Bullet Journal today. See if it works for you, and decide whether or not it's worth the investment.

Having a consecutive record of your daily life, from dreams to plans to goals, will become invaluable to you as you look back on the previous year(s) and remember all of the little things that made your life great.

# SPEED BUMPS

Road Trip Rule # 45:

Bring your own sunshine.

## The Quest

It seemed impossible and inexplicable that I continued to breathe after Mom's death. She'd always been my cheerleader, my therapist, the reliable and non-judgmental witness to my various victories and mistakes. I felt less solid. I had a sense of fading like the image in an old Polaroid picture.

I lived inside a fog so thick it weighed me down. My leaden arms and legs forgot how to operate, and most mornings I couldn't remember why it was so important that I wake up. Every day, I had to learn how to stand upright and walk all over again. My grief felt like a satchel full to bursting with sorrow and anguish, heavy as a wrecking ball and twice as unwieldy.

I'm still not sure how I functioned at work or at home (maybe I didn't). An overwhelming sadness commandeered my body and brain, carrying with it the sense of a marble slab wedged inside my rib cage in the space my heart had formerly occupied. Sometimes I'd cry loudly and messily, sometimes I'd throw up my lunch, sometimes I'd simply sit and stare while tears dripped down my face and landed in my lap. And still the invisible, thunderous clock ticked.

*It's later than you think.*

In an attempt to stop the incessant ticking and divert my mind, I ramped up the search for my dream motorhome.

My favorite website became rvtrader.com, which I checked daily. I also trolled the new listings on Craigslist and Camping World. Occasionally, I'd find a dealership in Iowa or Oregon or Texas and follow their inventory for a while. At least eight salespeople from eight different states emailed me regularly. An entire section of my Bullet Journal was dedicated to Class B Motorhomes and their various features, prices, and locations. (See the next Wayside for

Motorhome Class information.)

I established a custom search for my list of criteria that would alert me when such a vehicle became available. Soon, a constant symphony of pings, trills, chimes, and dings emanated from my phone. The minute I awoke each morning I checked my RV websites. Additional Google searches linked me to dealers around the country. I haunted owners' forums and read reviews, pored over various floor plans, and joined RV groups on Facebook.

Growing desperate, I increased my budget to $30,000. I wasn't sure how I'd conjure up the additional funds, but my misgivings were mere whispers compared to the relentless ticking. The obsession became all-consuming.

I registered with two websites and signed up for notifications if any rigs meeting my requirements and price range entered the market. My shopping list was specific: I wanted something small—less than twenty-two feet long—with a kitchenette, a fixed bed/couch that I wouldn't have to make up each night, and a dry bathroom. (Pause at the next Wayside—Head of the Class—for an explanation of wet and dry bathrooms.)

I also wanted a rig with good gas mileage. Diesel engines usually get better mileage than gas engines, so I searched for both types. Sometimes the mileage was included in the listings. Diesel engines tend to last longer than gas engines, too, so I didn't restrict my search criteria to a low odometer reading.

In a perfect world, my rig would be less than ten years old but I expanded my search to include rigs up to fifteen years old.

I found a dealership in Ohio with a Class B van motorhome, but a CarFax search revealed it had been wrecked and repaired. The salesman claimed to have no knowledge of the wreck (I didn't tell him I'd already researched it by VIN), and I crossed that dealership off the list. I found another in Iowa, but when I called, the van had already been sold. The one in Wisconsin sold before I called, too.

The popularity of these vans encouraged me to narrow my focus to a pinpoint and increase my search frequency.

One morning, while brushing my teeth, I refreshed the search on my phone and found a Class B motorhome with all of my preferred features packaged as a 2004 Mercedes Benz diesel van with a 2005 Forest River house. Nineteen feet of rust-free comfort with a full bathroom, a small dinette, a couch/bed, and a kitchen area. It had an onboard generator, an air conditioner, and a cube-shaped refrigerator as well as a microwave and two propane burners.

I was in love. Its official title was a Forest River MB Cruiser, but I already knew its real name: the Jan Van.

I called the dealer, Joel, and requested more information. It was still owned by the original owner, who had recently decided to upgrade. They were eager to sell. The asking price was \$32,000. I requested more photos, specifically of the undercarriage and engine, which Joel provided. A friend of mine perused the photos and researched that particular engine. The van had 140,000 miles on it, but these engines typically travel well over 250,000 miles, so that wasn't a concern.

Joel said it was still in stock. We chatted several times over the next couple of days. He measured the couch and the dinette for me; he checked the tire treads; he checked the oil. He started the on-board generator and ran it for a few hours. Or so he said.

I finally made an offer and spent the next day and a half pacing and wringing my hands. What if they didn't accept my offer? What if they *did*? I couldn't decide which outcome to hope for.

After work, I walked along the beach to burn some nervous energy. I was watching the whitecaps on Lake Huron when Joel called.

"The sellers accepted your offer." He sounded like he was grinning. I pictured him in a nondescript office, photos of his wife and kids on the battered walnut-laminate desk, a calendar blotter with my name and number scribbled in the corner.

I gave Joel my credit card information for the down payment and we discussed possible dates for me to take possession. The van had spent its first twelve years in Florida, far away from the corrosive salt scattered on the winter roads in Michigan's Upper Peninsula. I'd fly down to retrieve the Jan Van and drive it home over Labor Day weekend.

"One more question," I said. "If I get down there and I don't like it for whatever reason…"

"We'll refund your deposit. Every cent. You'll only be out a trip to Florida," Joel assured me.

After we ended the call my gaze returned to Lake Huron. I counted one hundred waves while I adjusted to my new status as fearless female solo road tripper.

I headed home to book a one-way ticket to Orlando.

# Wayside Ahead:
# Head of the Class

Motorhomes fall into three main categories: Class A, Class B, and Class C; and two subcategories: Class B+ and Super C.

## Class A

Class A motorhomes are the most expensive and luxurious of the three classes. They're built on a sturdy steel bus-style chassis and feature a billboard-sized front windshield and boxy body. Many Class A rigs don't have a passenger door next to the passenger seat—they can be entered only through the driver's door or the house door, which is typically located behind the passenger seat. The driver and passenger seats usually swivel around to face the house for additional seating while parked.

Class As are classy in every way imaginable: some have several slide-outs, master suites, two or three bathrooms, and laundry rooms outfitted with washers and dryers. Climbing into one is an elevating experience—a five-step staircase delivers you to the front of the house, usually in the kitchen/living area.

They might be trimmed in cherry wood or hickory, with full-sized refrigerators and granite countertops in their gourmet kitchens. Giant flat-screen televisions hang on living room walls above fireplaces and there's enough storage space below the floor to carry a fleet of kayaks or a couple of smart cars. Most Class A rigs sleep at least six; some sleep ten or twelve when you tally the regular beds, bunk beds, fold-out couches, convertible dinettes, convertible front seats and recliners designed to lie flat.

I've lived in houses smaller than some of the Class A motorhomes, which can be up to forty-five feet long. In my opinion, there should be a special driver's license required to pilot one of these mobile mansions on the public street, but anyone with a regular operator's license can legally climb behind the wheel with no additional training. Speaking of the wheel, the steering wheel is gigantic—like that in an eighteen-wheeler—and it's a stretch to settle your hands at ten and two, even with the multi-directional seat positioning system that seems comfortable enough to lull one to sleep. The seat is large enough to accommodate me in the fetal position.

A few Class A models are propelled by gas engines, but most of them are diesel-powered, and many are diesel pushers, with the engine tucked beneath the floor near the rear of the vehicle. It pushes, rather than pulls, the bus-sized palace forward.

Class A motorhomes ride fairly close to the

ground. They're built for long-haul travel on highways and Interstates, oversized for crowded city streets, and nearly impossible to park in urban areas. These limitations lead most Class A owners to tow auxiliary vehicles behind their rigs, so they can park at the campground or a shopping complex outside town and sightsee in their smaller vehicle. The luxury doesn't end at the back bumper of a Class A: most of the towed vehicles (commonly called "toads") are late model full-sized pick-up trucks or SUVs.

These high-end accommodations come with gold-plated price tags. A quick Google search led me to an article titled "How Much Does a Class A RV Cost?" at camperreport.com, which lists various models ranging in price from $120,468 to $907,842 before adding options. Despite the sky high price and sense of privilege these rigs boast, some of them don't include propane tanks, generators, or batteries (these add-ons can cost $2000 - $4000).

The model names of the elite fleet of Class As include the Palazzo, the Tuscany, and the Hurricane. The titles alone connote a certain apartness, an upper class-ness. A privileged prestige.

# Class B

Alphabetically, the Class B follows the Class A, but it's the smallest of the three classes. Class Bs are marketed to those who tend toward adventure; those more interested in experiences than in material wealth, who long to advertise their minimalist tendencies by taking extended vacations and/or living in their tiny rigs. If Class As are the RV equivalent of luxury condominiums, Class Bs are the tiny houses.

Class B motorhomes are basically vans with living quarters. Conversion vans, camper vans, and any van retro-fitted with camping facilities fit into this category. The iconic flower-bedecked Volkswagen is a perfect example. Some have pop-up roofs to increase living space; some have canvas fold-out beds or slide-outs; some Class B models manage to fit within the original van walls. Sizes range from fifteen to twenty-two feet in length, bumper to bumper. The standard amenities include a two-burner propane stove, microwave oven, cube-shaped refrigerator, convertible dinette and/or convertible couch, and a bathroom, which might be dry or wet.

A dry bathroom has a dedicated shower stall with a curtain or door to prevent water from flooding the bathroom. Dry bathrooms usually feature ample counter space and a mirrored medicine cabinet mounted to the wall.

A wet bathroom is one that converts into a shower stall. Typically, the shower head is mounted on the wall of the bathroom. To take a shower, one must remove a floor panel to reveal the drain, draw the curtain or shut the door, and take a shower. Everything in the bathroom gets wet. This doesn't appeal to me—I don't want to move the toilet paper and all of the other daily supplies I keep on the bathroom counter every time I take a shower. Most wet bathrooms have very little storage space and virtually no counter space. They're like slightly oversized airplane bathrooms with a shower feature. I eliminated many vans from my list immediately because of the wet bathroom on the floor plan. Wet bathrooms are popular because of their diminutive size, space being a premium commodity in a microscopic living space.

Unique options available in Class B vans include solar panels, a power awning, an office workspace, and an interior height of 75 inches. There are several small companies who will build out a van to an owner's specifications, and these bespoke mobile dwellings are quickly gaining popularity among Millennials and solo travelers.

Many Class Bs have onboard generators, making them fully self-contained. These rigs are nimble enough—some even have four-wheel drive—for boondocking on back roads (visit the Wayside following Mile Sixteen to read about boondocking), and spacious enough to carry adequate supplies for one or two people for a few days.

One might expect a Class B to sport a price tag to match its size, but brand new models can cost anywhere from $80,000 to $200,000. The bespoke versions can range in price as far as their owners' imaginations and budgets allow.

There's also a sub-category slivered between the B and C, called the Class B+. The differences are few but significant: the B+ is built on a van chassis, but the van body behind the cab is cut away and replaced with a slightly wider box-shaped dwelling. Because the van body is removed, the installed door operates like a typical camper door with an insulated exterior door and a screened interior door, usually with dead bolt locks and automatic steps that extend when the door is opened (the steps can be locked so they remain out, and automatically retract when driving). The B+ has a bubble-shaped protrusion above the cab that usually holds a flat screen television, and the front seats swivel around for additional seating when parked.

The small increase in size from a B to a B+ exponentially expands the floor plan options. Many Class B+ models feature Queen-sized beds and spacious dry bathrooms.

Diligent shoppers will find Class B+ models priced as low as $60,000, with an upper range around $180,000.

# Class C

Class C models are frequently called mini-motorhomes. They're medium-sized, typically with lengths from around twenty to twenty-eight feet. Built on a van chassis and retro-fitted with a boxy house similar to the B+, they are characterized by the bunk area above the cab, which increases the sleeping capacity without sacrificing floor space. Traditional Class C features include a "house door", similar to those found on B+ motorhomes, rather than the factory-issued sliding or two-part van door on the Class Bs. The most popular type of motorhome, Class Cs are easy to drive because of their low center of gravity. They can accommodate up to six or eight people.

Features include a convertible dinette, a fold-out couch, a dedicated sleeping space, and perhaps a slide-out or two. A typical Class C kitchen boasts a mid-sized refrigerator, a microwave, two or three propane burners, and maybe an oven large enough to bake a pizza. The over-cab sleeping quarters extends above the cab roof, and it can be converted to a pantry or storage area if additional accommodations aren't needed.

Prices start around $50,000 for a model fresh off the line, and they can extend beyond $100,000.

Those craving more power under the hood can explore the Super C option. The Super C offers the over-cab sleeping quarters like the Class C and many luxury amenities found in Class A motorhomes, built on a heavy duty commercial diesel truck chassis, such as a Ford F550. These rigs combine elegance and raw power. I don't see many Super Cs in my travels, maybe because their prices line up with those of Class As.

Those not yet ready to commit to a motorhome can rent one. Search the internet for RV rentals to find temporary rolling accommodations and take a road-tripping test drive.

# NO U-TURNS

Road Trip Rule # 53:

Take a chance
and hope for the best.

# Florida

I purchased a one way ticket from the local airport to Orlando. My stomach fluttered with anticipation— I'd traveled alone a few times as a kid, when I flew to visit my Aunt Karen, but she met me at the other end. It was predictable. I'd also traveled with my husband and children, but every trip had been highly structured. We had itineraries, reservations, solid plans.

This trip, however, had no itinerary, no reservations, and no plan beyond driving the van off the dealer's lot, which was over 2000 miles from home, and heading north toward the UP. Alone. It was the most exciting and spontaneous thing I had ever done, and I was doing it by myself. I felt empowered and brimming with the joyous confidence that I would return home a victorious traveler and brand new owner of an extremely used micro-house on wheels.

My local airport is quite small. It has one gate and a handful of employees, some of whom issue boarding passes behind the counter, then move over to the security section to monitor the luggage we place on the conveyor belt.

My backpack glided through the x-ray machine and emerged on the other side; my carry-on suitcase needed special attention.

"Step over here, please." The agent gestured to an empty section of counter. "I need to unzip your bag."

"That's fine." I smiled at her, but she was intent on her search.

She pulled out a small cast iron frying pan. "This is the culprit. I can't say I've ever seen anyone travel with a frying pan." Her gaze finally met mine.

"I'm flying down to Florida to pick up a motorhome." I shrugged. "And trying to be frugal."

She rummaged around in the bag again and pulled out my small stainless steel percolator.

"No knives?"

I shook my head no. "Just a cutting board. I'll buy a knife when I get there," I said.

She laughed. "Okay by me. Go ahead and repack your bag and take a seat."

I changed planes in Detroit and Washington Dulles— both layovers provided good opportunities to stretch my legs and guzzle some Starbucks. As if I needed coffee—I was fueled by anticipation and anxiety. In Orlando, we circled the airport for an additional twenty minutes before we were permitted to land. I was glad I only had carry-on bags and wouldn't waste time lingering at baggage claim.

Finally on the ground, I texted Joel as we'd arranged. He answered immediately. He was outside. My luggage weighed more than I did—I strapped my backpack to my small suitcase and wheeled them through the airport, careful not to let them tip over.

At long last, I stepped into the afternoon heat. Joel was parked at the curb, as promised, in a white Chevrolet Tahoe. He handed me a bottled water as we pulled away.

I expected a standard salesman chat, wherein Joel might ask about me and talk about the great deal I was getting on the van, but he surprised me. He told me about the two tours he'd completed in Iraq. He would be deployed again sometime in the following month. He worked at the RV dealership because the owners accommodated his schedule. He had a wife and two year old son, who didn't want him to go away again. But he told his boss he wanted to go because he felt called. When his monologue ended, I thanked him for his service. The reason he dominated the conversation with personal details didn't occur to me until much later, when I realized he'd been distracting me from asking questions.

We arrived at Alliance Coach just shy of 4:00 PM. Joel parked in front and took me inside. The sign on the door said they closed at 6:00.

"Where's the van?" I asked.

I was eager to see my new rig. I had envisioned this moment for months, traveled 2000 miles from home, and I was ready to begin my adventure. My goal was to stay near Savannah, Georgia, 260 miles away, that night.

The second hand on the clock swept forward without concern for my timetable. I had assumed that when I arrived at the dealership, I'd find the papers in a neat stack, pen ready for me to sign, the van itself polished and fueled and ready to roll.

"They're preparing it. They're nearly finished." Joel showed me where to find the restroom and refreshments.

Now I realize this was the first red flag: they'd had nearly a month to prepare the van—it should've been ready and waiting for me. But I'd been focusing on my Jan Van dream for so long, I barely registered the crimson banner in my peripheral vision.

After spending two hours perched on a vinyl chair in the corner of the waiting room, I grew antsy. I found Joel and said, "I need to see the van *now*."

We walked around the side of the building where my van was sitting. I circled the van, my critical eye trained on its form, and it looked perfect. A few scratches here and there, but considering it was twelve years old, it was pristine. He slid the side door open for me to go in.

"Don't be alarmed," he said. "It had a water hose break this morning, and we are drying it out. We replaced the water hose so it won't happen again."

I didn't recognize this for what it was: the second red flag. I didn't stop to question why he hadn't told me this in the first place, or wonder how much information was inaccurate or missing. I didn't even realize this was probably the reason he'd not mentioned the van on our drive from the airport.

A wiry man was vacuuming the carpeting in the van, and the air conditioner rattled overhead. The generator growled beneath the floor. When he finally stepped out, I got my first real look at the interior. It had some wear and tear, which I had expected from the photos. Joel assured me everything worked, and I was eager to get on the road. The technician shut off the air conditioner and generator, and I piloted it around the parking lot for a few minutes before hopping back out and declaring, "I'll take it."

After signing the papers and returning to the driver's seat, I paused long enough to make sure I knew how to start the generator. I asked one of the salesmen to show me what to do, and he showed me the button on the inside of the van that started the generator. He also showed me the button on the generator itself, in case the remote start didn't work for some reason. I pushed the remote start button, and I could hear it trying to start, but it wouldn't roll over. This happened several times, so I went back inside and told the salesman it wouldn't start.

He opened the outside panel to access the generator and said, "You just have to stick your hand in here and cover this hole while you're hitting the start button." He said this as if it was standard operating procedure.

*What?* I thought. *Why would I stick my hand inside an engine while it's running?* This was the third red flag, again ignored by me.

"Let it run for a few hours while you're driving down the road. Leave the air conditioner on so the generator has some load to carry. It'll clear itself out. It just hasn't been run in a while."

That sounded easy enough, I thought.

He filled my propane tank and I was off, misgivings firmly tamped and tucked.

The first thing I noticed, as I merged onto the freeway, was the burned out left turn signal. Thankfully, the van easily accelerated to match the speed of traffic, but how in the world would I drive all the way home with only one blinker?

Why, oh why, had I not checked the headlights, taillights, and blinkers? I'll tell you why: when you purchase a vehicle from a dealership, no matter how old it is, the dealer should check all of those components for you. The bigger issue is, if the small things like blinkers aren't maintained, the more critical things probably aren't maintained, either. The vermilion banners finally entered my consciousness but I held them at a virtual arm's length, unwilling to admit the Jan Van was anything less than fabulous.

I considered turning around, but that would have cost me a minimum of another hour, if anyone still remained at the dealership. I'd stayed beyond their regular business hours to address the generator issues, and I assumed the employees had left when I did.

The rearview mirror in the center of the windshield reflected the living quarters. Rather unhelpful. My next disconcerting realization was that I couldn't see out of the passenger side mirror without scootching to the right and craning my entire body over so far I strained my seatbelt and nearly toppled into the passenger seat. I adjusted the mirror but my view didn't improve.

The cruise control, on a separate lever on the steering column, seemed to be out of commission. I twisted, pushed, and pulled, but nothing happened.

So. I would have to drive 2000 miles with no left rear blinker, no cruise control, and a nearly unusable passenger side mirror. This van was more like the Rolls K'Nardly (and less like the van of my dreams) than I'd anticipated.

The traffic rushed me northward.

The day's events suddenly gathered together and

hit me with everything—the early alarm, the three flights, no proper meals, disappointing revelations at the dealership, and the $28,000 expenditure—and left me overwhelmed and exhausted. No time for that now, I told myself. I gripped the wheel and monitored the traffic and listened to the squeaks, creaks, and groans behind me. The generator provided a constant bass tone to the cacophony.

When I'd plugged in the GPS at the dealership, I programmed the address for the Jacksonville Walmart so I could buy everything on my list before settling in for the night. Prior to the trip, I had researched various places that allowed RVs to park overnight for free, and the Jacksonville Walmart offered this courtesy. It had looked and sounded easy as I sat on the couch at home gazing at the map. However, I hadn't factored in my uneasiness in a new van or the unfamiliar city.

The sun was setting as I pulled into the Walmart lot and shut off the van. I sat there listening to the generator for a few minutes, waffling about leaving it running or shutting it off. I finally decided to shut it off, as it had been running for over two hours, and I didn't want to leave it running when I wasn't there. Not that I'd know what to do if something went wrong, but it seemed irresponsible to leave it running unattended.

The remote stop button worked to shut the generator off. I crossed my fingers that it would start again, and stepped out of the van and into the liquid heat of the Florida evening. People shouted taunts and threats at each other across the parking lot.

I locked the side door before sliding it shut, then clicked the key fob to lock the front doors. It sounded like the doors locked, then unlocked. I clicked it again and they locked, then unlocked again. I didn't want to try the door and advertise my lack of security, so I glanced around and no one seemed to be paying any attention. I calmly walked toward the store, hoping the van wouldn't be invaded while I shopped.

The store's fluorescent light haze contributed to my sense of bewilderment. Blue-vested associates nodded at me as I cruised the aisles and found everything on my list. There's something surreal about shopping on a road trip at night. The store is an odd blend of the familiar—I know the floor plan—and the unfamiliar—Southern-relevant stock items like grits and canned okra and the singsong twang of the customers and store clerks.

When I approached the van with my full shopping bags I tried the door without clicking the key fob and it opened. What good was a key fob that couldn't lock the doors?

I unpacked my groceries and tossed the rest of my items on the bed. The insidious heat and humidity had already oozed into the van. I crossed my fingers and pressed the remote start button, but the generator just chugged and chuckled, refusing to turn over. There were two other motorhomes and one ramshackle travel trailer parked nearby, and disembodied voices continued to jeer and torment each other across the parking lot. Sleeping in a parking lot suddenly seemed beyond my mettle and I yearned for a site at a proper campground.

One of my camping apps showed vacancy at a KOA campground about a mile up the road. They offered after-hours check-in for $42 per night, and I stuffed cash in the envelope at the registration office and selected my site. I left the van only long enough to plug in the electrical cord.

The temperature dropped with the sun, and I was grateful I'd decided to postpone my parking lot sleepover experience. I plugged in the electric heater and unwrapped the pillow I'd purchased at Walmart and shoved it into the pillowcase from my carry-on bag. I unrolled the blanket I'd brought and made up the bed, and exchanged my skirt for a pair of pajama pants.

My head buzzed, a whirlwind of detail detritus. Had I made a mistake, spending so much money? Would I be able to learn everything I needed to know about the van? How many more things would I discover didn't work properly?

Was this my midlife crisis?

I pulled out my log book—a fresh notebook in which I planned to record my Jan Van travels—and wrote my first entry. I noted the odometer reading and a few of the needed repairs and summed up the day's adventures.

There was no way I could fall asleep yet, so I lit the

burner and heated some water for tea. The van felt cozy with the electric heater blowing and the interior lights on. I glanced toward the cockpit and noted the door lock buttons were still lit. I double-checked the doors—they were locked.

As I sipped my tea, I pulled out my Bullet Journal and made a list of things I needed to figure out or fix.

1. Door locks - do they work?
2. Left rear blinker - replace
3. Cruise control - how to use
4. Generator - find mechanic
5. New headlights or headlight polishing kit
6. Additional key
7. Install board beneath bed

I made a second list of things to update or replace.

1. Sew new curtains for front windows
2. Replace carpeting with hard flooring
3. Replace bathroom faucet with taller one
4. Install roof vent hood/cover
5. Sew new cushion covers for dinette
6. Find cover for propane burners to increase counter space
7. New shower curtain
8. Paint cabinets

As usual, leaving some of my worries on the page settled my mind. I sat at the table with the atlas spread open, rechecking my intended route to Savannah. The dinette table was a bit wobbly—it was a pedestal table, and it sloped to one side with any weight or movement. I'd need to secure it to the wall somehow —another thing for my list. I finished my tea and brushed my teeth, carefully rinsing my toothbrush, which barely fit beneath the stubby bathroom faucet.

The bed was comfortable—I had plenty of space to stretch out. The bed itself was a metal frame with a thick cushion affixed to it. The bed was actually a couch, but the back cushions were missing. Below the bed, the twenty-five gallon fresh water tank and water filter were stowed. The water lines snaked throughout the compartment to supply the bathroom at the back of the rig and the kitchen toward the front.

I was hyperaware of the gaps between the bed and the wall—my irrational fear of mice and other small rodents enlarged these gaps to nightmarish proportions, and in my mind's eye they were inviting portals through which a conga line of mice could easily enter. I planned to install a hinged trap door beneath the mattress that would eliminate the disturbing gaps but still allow access to the fresh water tank.

Huddled under the thin blanket I'd packed, I slept intermittently—the fridge and its rhythmic belch and purr interrupted my slumber every hour or so. Sometime around 2:00 AM, I rose and shut it off.

The moonlight did not penetrate the blackout blinds, and the campground was quiet after I silenced the fridge. I climbed back into bed and drifted off, finally relaxing my mind and unclenching my muscles.

The next morning, my confidence returned with the sun. I used the campground shower house, hopped back into the van and brewed a steaming hot pot of coffee, and set off toward Savannah, Georgia.

Road Trip Rule # 97:

Wherever you go, there you are.

# Wayside Ahead:
# Hook-Ups

When I first started camping, I noticed some campgrounds advertise sites with "electric only" or "electric and water". These terms are self-evident: there's a short post with a 20-amp, 30-amp, or 50-amp outlet near the edge of the site, and there may also be a short post with a water spigot at the edge of the site.

Then I encountered the term full hook-ups, which I assumed was a neater way to say "electric and water". After all, what else can be hooked up?

Full hook-ups include water, electric, sewer, and sometimes cable television. You can wash dishes, take showers, and bake cookies while running the air conditioner and watching the game.

Full hook-ups are the holy grail of the camper who plans to spend several days in one campsite. Full hook-ups let a camper experience residential life in the campground.

The Jan Van is self-contained—it doesn't need any hook-ups to function. If I want to run the microwave or air conditioner, or if I desire to use more power than my inverter can provide, I run the generator.

With a full tank of fresh water, I can live without hook-ups for several days before emptying my waste tanks and refilling my water tank.

Road Trip Rule # 16:

With enough coffee, you can drive through anything.

## Georgia To Virginia

I hit the Jacksonville morning rush hour and arrived in Savannah around noon.

I parallel parked the van after circling a couple of blocks in search of a safe place to leave my new investment. The day was heavy and humid as I walked the Savannah streets. A world away from Orlando, Savannah's arching foliage canopy invited me to slow down and enjoy the enchanting neighborhood.

Shopkeepers greeted me as I entered their air conditioned stores. I found an artisanal chocolate shop, a bookstore, a clothing store, and several interesting boutiques. I fought the urge to linger—there were far too many miles between me and home for prolonged dillydallying.

I set off from Savannah around 3:30 PM and continued northward. Soon, fat raindrops spattered my windshield. I was relieved to discover my wipers worked. When I passed through Spartanburg, South Carolina, the clouds cleared and the sun resumed its regular position.

The needle on the fuel gauge hovered below the quarter-tank mark.

I pulled into a truck stop and parked at the diesel pump on the driver's side. I hopped out and walked toward the back of the van, searching for the fuel cap. The only visible cap was for the fresh water intake. I opened the generator panel—no fuel cap there. I stood back and scanned my eyes slowly over the length of the van. Nothing.

Mindful of the dirty fuel pumps—I wore a bright pink skirt, sandals, and a cream-colored tank top—I walked around the vehicle twice, willing the fuel cap to appear. I circled the vehicle a third time, and still couldn't find it. Finally, I pulled the owner's manual out, flipping pages frantically.

That's when I noticed a trucker a couple of bays away watching me and chuckling. He stood next to his truck in stained blue overalls, a brutal contrast to my inappropriate attire.

According to my owner's manual, the fuel cap was right inside the driver's door, which I'd closed to look for the fuel cap. Expecting the cap to be farther back on the van, I had pulled about twelve feet too far forward. To spite the chuckling trucker, who appeared to be wiping tears of laughter from his eyes, I didn't reposition the van. I grabbed the pump and pulled and pulled the large, heavy hose, holding it away from my body, until it finally reached the van and blackened my hands. I flipped the lever. Nothing happened.

I cleaned my hands with an antibacterial wipe, then walked inside and asked the pimply child behind the counter to turn on the diesel pump.

"You have to leave your credit card here while you pump." He flicked his greasy hair out of his eyes. "I'll give it back to you after you pay for the fuel."

I returned to the van, grabbed my credit card, and ran back inside. The cashier turned the pump on and I filled the tank. By this time, the trucker was enjoying a full belly laugh. This was probably the best show he had seen in quite a few miles. He gestured to two other drivers who walked toward him so they could have a better view. I now had an entire audience.

The fuel tank finally full, I paid and retrieved my credit card and quickly glanced at my clothes and legs —no dirty smears. I climbed back into the driver's seat and grinned at the short line of truckers as I pulled out of the truck stop.

Road construction crews had closed all but one

lane for several miles of highway, and I bounced along between a semi-truck hauling frozen vegetables and a pickup truck towing a camper trailer. The road signs warned us about the narrow lane, made narrower by potholes and toppled orange cones. The road workers themselves seemed oblivious to traffic —they operated cranes and walked mere inches from the cones.

*This road represents my life*, I thought. One lane only, narrow and battered, broken edges, debris littering the margins. Traffic doesn't stop for a broken road and life doesn't stop for a broken heart.

I'd already driven the first mile on my own road to recovery by purchasing the Jan Van. My travel dreams were becoming a reality and I'd soon be a confident solo road-tripper. The van needed some small repairs and updates, but the engine was strong and reliable.

The road itself transitioned to blemish-free asphalt after a few miles, and the traffic resumed its regular pace. This seemed to further illustrate my life-under-construction metaphor and I felt infused with hope for my own future.

I drove on.

When I finally reached the Blue Ridge Parkway, fog shrouded everything. I'd traveled portions of it with Jason twice before, both times in thick fog. Sometimes the fog loomed close, and sometimes it lingered a few hundred feet from the scenic turnouts. This time, it blanketed everything. Visibility was about thirty feet.

The Blue Ridge Parkway, also known as America's Favorite Drive, was built in the Depression Era to connect Shenandoah National Park to the Great Smoky Mountains National Park. The winding 469-mile-long stretch of two-lane blacktop posts a top speed of 45 miles per hour and offers access to mountain vistas, hiking, biking, and equestrian trails, waterfalls, campgrounds, and several communities. There are tourist sites, State Parks, visitor centers, picnic areas, restaurants, and fishing streams.

The fog had thinned a little by the time I reached Grandfather Mountain, a North Carolina State Park that features the highest swinging bridge in America, spanning an 80-foot gorge a mile above sea level. I turned onto the steep entrance road and tuned my radio to the Grandfather Mountain station to listen to the spiel as I entered the park. At 5,946 feet, Grandfather Mountain is the highest peak on the eastern escarpment of the Blue Ridge Mountains. It was named by Hugh Morton, who inherited the land from his grandfather and built the swinging bridge as a tourist attraction. Morton passed away in 2006, and North Carolina purchased the land two years later for $12 million. The State Park was officially established in 2009. There are eleven hiking trails, some of which offer the most rugged and intense hiking experiences in the Eastern US.

No other vehicles shared the road during my climb, which gave me a bit of centerline leeway around the hairpin curves, one of which featured a sign reading 'Forrest Gump ran this curve'. I climbed and climbed and climbed, and finally arrived at the parking lot.

I wandered through the visitors' center, waiting for the fog to dissipate, but it refused to reveal anything beyond the edge of the parking lot. I purchased a ticket and walked across the bridge and along part of a hiking trail in the eerie, foggy stillness, then returned to the van. Grandfather Mountain remained cloaked.

I continued northward on the Blue Ridge Parkway for a while, enjoying the slow pace and sparse traffic, mentally commiserating with Jason about the relentless fog. I pulled over at one of the scenic turnouts and made lunch, again unable to out-wait the fog that curtained the view.

After a while, I exited the Parkway and came upon Wytheville (pronounced With-ville), Virginia. Discovering towns like this is my favorite part of road tripping: a main street lined with funky shops, friendly people, and interesting sights. I took a photo of the Wytheville Office Supply store and its gigantic pencil suspended above the sidewalk. Wytheville boasts a robust entertainment calendar dotted with festivals and live performances as well as several museums and parks.

I found a campground with a vacant full-hookup site for $25 on my ParkAdvisor app, and called the number listed.

"Shady Acres Camp-N-Go, this is Becky." A screen door slammed in the background as she spoke.

"Good afternoon, Becky. This is Jan Kellis. Do you have any vacancy for tonight? I have a 20' Class B."

"Yep. Twenty-five bucks. Cash only." Becky spoke in a no-nonsense tone, a direct contrast to most campground receptionists who acted as if we were fast friends after three words of conversation.

"That's no problem," I said. "I just want to verify your address before I program my GPS." The app is fairly reliable, but I always verify.

She gave me the address, then said, "The road is hard to see. There's no road sign anymore, so watch for the rusty old red Ford truck. It's sitting in the weeds on the righthand side of the road. You'll want to turn right about fifty feet past that truck."

"Okay, thank—" My words disappeared as she resumed.

"And if you see the sign for Scooter's Honey, you've gone too far. Turn back and try again."

"That's a good tip, thanks! I'll be there in about an hour."

"Yeah. The sign shows a cartoon honeybee. It's embarrassing." She sighed. "After you turn, go down the hill, up the hill, down the hill, and up. We're at the top of that second hill, on the right. If you're going to be late, give us a call. Or if you're not coming, give us a call. We don't want to wait around here for nothing."

The app listed this campground with a five-star rating and there were several rave reviews about the sites, shower facilities, cost, and friendliness of staff.

I continued on. My GPS directed me to turn on the unmarked road just beyond the rusted out Ford truck. I was glad Becky had described the two hills for me—I would have missed their sign if I hadn't known where to look, and the GPS wanted me to continue on for another half mile.

I turned into Shady Acres and pulled up to a dirt-crusted modular house. The siding had broken in several places, revealing dusty silver insulation board behind it. Nothing was marked as an office and I couldn't see a campground anywhere. As I counted out $25, a woman opened the screen door of the house and waved me in. I left the van running and walked over.

Becky looked like I had pictured her from her voice on the phone. Tall and robust with short gray hair and an unsmiling face. She had a form already filled out with my name and site number, which she pushed across the counter to me.

"We gave you the best site. It overlooks the pond." She went on to tell me where the shower house was —I'd have to walk around the pond to reach it.

"Thank you." I smiled at her, but she wouldn't crack. I didn't know why I wanted her to like me, but I felt the need to somehow brighten her day. Perhaps it was a side effect of my midwest upbringing, or simply my mom's training in the social art of friendliness, but I suddenly needed a thread of connection. A glimmer of human understanding.

"This is my second night with this rig. I bought it a couple of days ago in Florida, and I'm driving home to Michigan."

She snorted. "Sounds like fun." Becky looked like she wouldn't recognize fun if it knocked on her door and called her sweetie pie, but I rambled on as if she cared, desperate for a positive reaction.

She didn't oblige.

"I drove up Grandfather Mountain this morning," I said. "I wish I had more time to enjoy this trip. There are so many things to see. Have you been to Wytheville? It's a—"

She waved my words away as if they were irritating houseflies. "I've been everywhere. It's overrated. Dave's outside waiting. He'll lead you to your site. You're going to drive around the pond—it's a one-way street so when you leave in the morning, continue the same way and you'll end up right back here."

I looked out the window as she talked, and saw a man on a golf cart next to the van. Two kids climbed into the back of the cart as I watched. Dirt streaked their skinny legs and arms. I thanked Becky again, paid her, and exited the building to join Dave and the kids.

They led me beyond the house and down the two-track that circled a stagnant pond partially covered in algae. The water looked dense, as if you could toss just about anything in there and it would immediately decompose. We drove at a sedate five miles per hour and I noticed another driveway branching off which led to three circa-1950 trailer houses perched on the side of a gentle slope. I counted five other campsites, all empty. Had I stumbled onto some kind of commune?

The sky was turning pink as Dave pulled through my site, demonstrating where I should park with wild gesticulations. The kids bailed out of the back of the golf cart and grabbed their bikes, which they'd apparently abandoned earlier, and raced around the pond.

I parked beneath the generous, leafy limbs of a willow tree and hopped out to hook up the electric cord and sewer hose, and Dave walked over.

"Did you pay Becky?" He shoved his hands into the pockets of his dirty jeans and focused on my forehead when he spoke.

What an odd question—was he trying to collect my camping fee twice? "Yes, I paid when I checked in. This is a beautiful place. How many campsites do you have?"

He pulled a set of keys from his pocket and jangled them. "A few. This is a side gig for us. We have jobs."

Becky had acted like I was an unwanted interruption, and now Dave seemed anxious and shifty. Was the campground a front for some less-than-legal endeavor?

The campsite was compact, and the water and sewer hoses both easily reached the hook-ups. I'd be able to shower in the van—I wouldn't need to brave the pre-dawn walk around the creepy-looking pond.

I hooked everything up while Dave talked.

His fidgeting made me nervous. The kids continued to circle the pond, legs pumping hard, tangled hair flowing out behind. Three more kids had appeared since I'd parked and they called to one another from their bikes.

Dave finally dropped his gaze and muttered something about letting him know if I needed anything. He shuffled back to the golf cart and drove toward the house.

Something wasn't quite right here, but I didn't feel unsafe. If the campground was a front for something else, I supposed I was helping their business appear legitimate. I didn't feel a full-blown uneasiness—it was more of a vague distrust. It was only one night, and I could drive away at a moment's notice if anything went awry.

If Jason had been traveling with me, I probably wouldn't have noticed Dave's oddness. I wouldn't have felt uneasy or unsure of myself. Traveling alone presented a new set of challenges. Every female has the innate ability to sense malicious intent from members of the opposite sex—a kind of threat-meter that compels us to react or retreat to protect ourselves. My threat-meter had been dormant while I was with Jason, and it was now hyperactive and spastic, spewing out inconsistent readings. I decided to stay as planned.

I still had some leftover salad, and I cooked a

couple of eggs to go with it. I ate outside beneath the tree while the sun painted the sky pink.

The kids raced around the pond past sunset, their constant banshee chatter punctuated by the recurring whoosh of bike tires whizzing past my campsite.

Finally, when it was too dim to see, someone yelled from one of the mobile homes perched on the slope behind me.

"Rusty! Luanne! All you kids! Get your asses to home!"

The kids scattered to their respective trailers and left the night to the crickets.

## Virginia To Michigan

The next morning, I woke early to take my first shower in the van. I turned on the water heater and made coffee while I waited for the water to reach a tolerable temperature. The shower curtain barely spanned the opening. Instead of using the channel and tiny hooks pre-installed with the shower unit, the previous owners had hung a regular shower curtain on large plastic hoops and cut the curtain to size, perhaps because they were unable to find one that fit.

The hot water restored my body and soul, but I fought the urge to linger in the shower. The water heater only held six gallons of water.

After getting dressed and blowdrying my hair, I decided to empty the black and gray tanks and refill the freshwater tank. I retrieved my rubber gloves from the trunk area and opened the black tank valve (pull over at the upcoming Wayside to learn more about black and gray tanks). When it finished draining, I opened the gray tank valve. I ran inside and flushed the toilet a few times to rinse out the black tank line a bit more, then closed both valves and stowed the hose in a big plastic bag the dealership had given me. It fit into the trunk area—a Fiberglas rectangle across the back of the van that housed the spare tire, the sewer hose, and a few small tools.

My twenty-five gallon freshwater tank, below the bed, was nearly empty. I shut off the water at the spigot, removed the hose from the van's "city water" hook-up, removed the pressure regulator from the hose, and shoved the hose into the freshwater intake. RV plumbing systems are networks of flexible plastic tubing, and are rated for a maximum of 40psi water pressure. Water spigots, however, spew water with a force strong enough to destroy RV plumbing connections. A water pressure regulator can be purchased for less than ten dollars at a camping supply store, and should always be used when attaching a hose to an RV's "city water" connection. The regulator itself is a small device that screws onto the end of the hose, then connects to the camper.

Since the Jan Van's freshwater intake was a tube (not a screw-on connection), it didn't require a water hose pressure reducer and filled within ten minutes.

By the time I'd finished all of these chores, it was time to hit the road. The sun was threatening to rise and I wanted to arrive at my daughter Steph's, near East Lansing, Michigan, before dinner time. I unplugged the van, stowed the electrical cord, and did a final walk-around before entering through the sliding door and refreshing my coffee. I locked the sliding door and started the van.

I crossed from Virginia to West Virginia, then into Ohio and finally Michigan, through small towns, past farms, through cities, across bridges, and through a tunnel. The day was dedicated to putting miles behind me, and I wished I had time to explore some of the scenic lookouts, hiking trails, and funky little shops that I sped past. The van handled the mountains pretty well, and I easily kept up with traffic as we wound up, over and through the beautiful farmlands and over gorges and rivers.

This was my third day driving the van and I was happy to note it was a comfortable ride. The passenger mirror continued to trouble me, although I now had my maneuver down to a science. I scooted an inch or two over to the right, extended my left leg out for balance, craned my neck, then quickly diverted my eyes from the road to the mirror. It wasn't perfect, but it worked.

I fueled up again somewhere in Ohio and calculated my mileage at 22 miles per gallon. So far, I'd driven through a few road construction projects, torrential rain, high winds, and two sizable cities during rush hour. I'd parallel-parked in Savannah and figured out how to use the cruise control somewhere along the way. I still had no idea how to lock the doors with the key fob, but I could lock the front doors from the inside and exit through the sliding door, locking it on my way out.

Buoyed by these small victories, I drove on. If I didn't glance directly at the passenger seat, I could half-convince myself my mom was riding shotgun, sharing my big adventure and cheering me on. She would've commented on my bravery and told me she was glad she wasn't the one driving through the high-traffic and high-speed areas. Mom had loved a good road trip, but she was most comfortable driving back and forth across the UP, where the towns were small and traffic sparse.

Rotund gray and white clouds kept a lid on the day along most of my route, but somewhere in southeast Ohio a slanted column of sunlight beamed on the farmland ahead. I took a deep breath and kept my focus on the road. When I was a child, Mom and I had been at the beach one cloudy day when a beam of sunlight suddenly shot down and sparkled on the water a few hundred yards off shore. "That's my favorite phenomenon," Mom had said. "It's Mother Nature's spotlight."

If there is such a thing as heaven, and if it's located in the clouds, maybe the angels take turns controlling various phenomena. Maybe today it was Mom's turn.

I arrived at Steph's mid-afternoon. She was still working, so I parked the van in the far parking lot of her apartment complex and walked down the block to the brewery where she tended bar. The brewery was a converted warehouse and featured a polished concrete floor and a high ceiling with exposed pipes. There were several tables and a long bar tucked in the corner, backed by a tall chalkboard menu announcing their various beers and ales on tap. Steph moved efficiently behind the bar, serving people and filling orders for the wait staff. Her long blonde hair was piled on top of her head in an artfully messy bun and she had a fresh French tip manicure. She looked happy and busy.

I visited with her coworkers and chatted with her while she finished her shift, then we walked back to tour the van.

"It looks kind of old," said Steph as we crossed the parking lot.

"It has 140,000 miles on it."

"Why did you buy something so old? And used?" She wrinkled her nose. "It's like, really used."

"Because it was $28,000. If I wanted something newer, I'd have to spend at least twice that."

"Wow, this was twenty-eight *grand?*"

I nodded.

I unlocked the front doors with the key fob, then reached in and unlocked the sliding door so she could enter. Watching her look into the van helped me view it with more objective eyes: the stained carpet, cracked countertop, scuffed cabinet doors, outdated upholstery, dented fridge. A need to defend the van's shabby appearance, as if it were a friend who'd arrived at a formal party wearing sweatpants, possessed me.

"I know it's banged up a bit, but it has potential."

"I see it—I see what you see," said Steph. She looked around slowly. "You can paint the cupboards, sew new cushion covers, steam clean the carpet."

"I'm going to replace the carpet with hard flooring of some kind."

She nodded. "Even better. And the countertop isn't too bad. You probably won't notice it after you do all of the updates. Those curtains are ugly, though." She pointed to the drab brown curtains slouching from tired velcro tabs above the windshield. "Those have to go, Mom."

Steph has always focused on aesthetics. Her high school English teacher had once assigned her to write a research paper about an influential historical figure and she'd called me immediately.

"She expects me to write about Einstein. Can you believe that? Einstein!" She was breathing fast.

I held the phone an inch away from my ear.

"What's wrong with Einstein? He led an interesting life. You'll figure out an angle—"

"Mom. Have you *seen* him? He looks like a lunatic."

I sighed. There was no talking her down over the phone. "Well—what are you going to do?"

"I told her I'd write about Marilyn Monroe."

"And she'll accept that?"

I could hear the grin in her voice. "Yep."

She got an A on that paper.

Now, she walked back and forth in the van, checking out the bathroom, opening cabinets, sitting at the dinette. "It's comfy in here," she said. "I could definitely live in this thing."

"I knew you were going to say that." I laughed.

Steph's apartment faced east and had an exterior entrance on the second floor. It featured a view of the parking lot on one side and the back side of a warehouse on the other side. Three apartments separated hers from the train that thundered past at odd hours, blowing its whistle to announce its approach to the intersection. Usually, when I stayed over, Steph's boyfriend slept on the couch so she and I could share the bed. I always offered to take the couch, but Steph insisted I was too old for that and I didn't argue.

At least once per month I'd drive down for the weekend and we'd go shopping, cook together, get pedicures, and walk around town or explore a trail she'd discovered since my previous visit. We knew where the best thrift stores were, and when they held sales. Her apartment showcased our favorite finds: a table lamp shaped like a woman clad in a 1920s-style dress, a long, narrow New York City skyline painting, an upholstered swivel chair. We cruised the estate sales, the yard sales, and the farmers markets. Our weekends were wall-to-wall laughter and adventure.

As it turned out, this was our last fun weekend together. When I returned a month later, I'd help her pack so she could move to Alaska to be closer to her sister Dani.

# Wayside Ahead:
# Black Tank

Many people ask about the black and gray tanks. The toilet drains into the black tank, and the sinks and shower drain into the gray tank. Some larger rigs have two gray tanks—one for the bathroom sink and shower, and one for the kitchen.

Draining the black tank sounds daunting. The possibility of a spill, a leak, or a smelly biohazard overwhelms people. Then there's the performance component of black tank emptying: more often than not, you'll be emptying it while the next camper waits behind you, watching your every move (or so it seems) through their gigantic windshield.

Managing the black tank for the summer—or longer, if you're a full-timer—is fairly straightforward. I used to think the black tank should be emptied every time I went away for a weekend, but after I bought my own rig, I studied several YouTube videos and learned most people empty their tanks too early and too often. The chemicals added to the black tank need time to work, and if there's only one person using it, the black tank might take nearly two weeks to fill.

When emptying tanks, remember to empty the

black tank first, then the gray tank. The tanks each have their own drain pipes, but they join together near the end, where the valves are located, so you only have to connect one drain hose to empty everything. Emptying the black tank first allows the gray water to rinse that last length of pipe.

To empty the tanks, remove the cover from the drain pipe near the rear of the rig and attach the sewer hose. Make sure the other end of it is securely inserted into the dump station tube. Open the valve for the black tank and let it drain completely. Flush the toilet a couple of times, or run water into the "black water rinse" hook-up if your RV has one, to rinse out the black tank. Open the gray tank valve and let it drain, then shut the black, then the gray valves before detaching the sewer hose from the RV. Rinse out the sewer hose—most dump stations offer a non-potable water hose for this purpose—and pack up.

The water hoses at dump sites are sometimes difficult to control because they're secured in a stiff coil of wire and when you pull them down low enough to use, you're fighting against that coil. Turn the rinse water on so it's a steady stream, but not a heavy blast of water. Beware of spatter!

Many people wear gloves while emptying the tanks. I used to, but now I simply wash my hands and wipe them with an antibacterial wipe immediately afterward. I keep the wipes and a spray bottle of cleaning solution in the storage bin near the valves. Some people rinse the various sewer components with rubbing alcohol, but I don't go to that length. Do whatever makes you feel comfortable. The black tank contains chemically-treated sewage, and the chemicals kill most of the bacteria.

I usually leave the campground early in the morning when the other campers are still sleeping, but once in a while someone pulls in behind me to watch my process. Rushing through this chore can result in a biohazard spill, so take your time and continue to be careful. Every RVer deals with this unpalatable bit of camping.

# Road Trip Rule # 4:

Travel slowly.
Enjoy every moment.

## Assumptions

The next day, the sunrise revealed a calm early autumn morning. Steph and I rented kayaks in downtown Lansing and paddled up and down the Grand River for a couple of hours, our way of bidding farewell to summer. There weren't many others out paddling—we had the river to ourselves. Steph's chihuahua, Milo, sat on her lap while she paddled.

From there, we drove to the Meridian Mall and ate lunch at Schuler's Chapbook Cafe, tucked into a front corner of my favorite bookstore. Schuler's sells new and used books and the cafe's menu is packed with interesting items like grilled artichoke paninis and various quiches. It's impossible to leave Schuler's without a happy stomach and a bag full of books.

After lunch we shopped our favorite consignment boutiques, then hiked one of the trails near the Meridian Mall. We grabbed a late afternoon snack at the brewery before her shift started, and I set off toward home when she clocked in.

The sun had set by the time I arrived at the Mom-and-Pop campground I'd found on my app. I could've driven all the way home—a mere four hours from Steph's—and saved myself the campsite fee, but I wasn't quite ready for the trip to end.

I walked into the office and talked to Jim, tall and thin with a receding hairline and robust mustache, no gray showing yet. He stood behind the counter monitoring the three young boys who were inspecting the ice cream selection.

"I'm the one who called a couple of hours ago," I said. "Class B, one night."

"Hello! Yes, you're in site 17." He slid a map across the counter with site 17 prominently highlighted. It was across the street from the office. "I know it says to drive around the block to park, but there's no traffic right now. Tell your husband to stop here, and back in from this direction." He pointed to the map.

The word 'husband' made me flinch. I swallowed hard. "He's—not—It's just me."

Jim shook his head once. "I'm sorry, I thought your husband sent you in." He smiled. "That's what most husbands do. They wait outside while their wives do the paperwork."

"That's what we used to do, too. But he's—no longer with me." I realized after I said it how it sounded, but it was too late to retract. White noise filled my ears and everything, myself included, suddenly seemed farther away. I took a deep breath and fought to remain upright. I gripped the edge of the counter and tried to focus on the third button on Jim's shirt.

They would call an ambulance if a person keeled over in their lobby—and what would I tell the paramedics? *I'm sorry, I can't seem to recover from this heartbreaking divorce, and it's easier for me to tell people he's no longer with me than that he no longer wanted to be married to me. And I miss my mom. She should be taking her own road trips, having adventures, living. I can't carry this much grief— it bogarts my oxygen and pulls a hood over my head and threatens to leave me in a heap on the floor.*

Grief was an overinflated balloon inside my chest, a divorce-sized airbag that simply couldn't hold enough air. I needed a larger receptacle—a blimp, maybe, or a zeppelin—to handle the pressure. Someone had turned on the grief-air and walked away while it filled the balloon in my chest and it kept hissing and hissing, deafening me and pumping air into the over-filled vessel until—what? If it burst would my heart explode? Would I no longer be able to function (or appear to function) and wake up days later in a mental ward? What did a full-on breakdown look like?

My hands still gripped the counter, gray skin and white knuckles. I shoved them into my jacket pockets.

"Oh! Oh, no." Jim clasped his hands near his heart.

The door behind Jim opened and a ponytailed woman glided in, dressed in running gear.

"Sylvie, Sylvie." Jim clutched her upper arm with one hand and gestured toward me with the other. "She's camping alone. She and her husband used to go camping, and he's deceased. But she still goes!"

Sylvie fixed her gaze on me and stepped to the counter to reach across and pat my arm. "You're so brave," she said. She looked up at Jim. "I'd do the same thing, you know." She stepped around Jim and punched buttons on the cash register.

Jim tilted his head, puppy-dog style, and looked at me. He spoke in a near whisper. "How long has he been gone?"

"Almost a year." I swallowed again. My face flushed in a hot wave of shame at my inability to utter the truth.

Jim reached across the counter to pat my shoulder. I was so surprised, I didn't step back.

"I'll come out and help you park your rig," he said.

"It's no problem. And I'm so glad you're still camping. You *are* brave."

Sylvie clutched the day's receipts in one hand, and cash and credit card slips in the other. "I'll watch the shop while you help her," she said.

"I know you can park it yourself." Jim grabbed a windbreaker and slid an arm into it. "But it's a narrow site, and it's much easier if someone is watching the back end for you."

"Thank you," I said.

Jim guided me into the site and stuck around while I installed the electric cord.

The only thing worse than gargantuan grief is sympathy. Sympathy is another person's way of attempting to shoulder a portion of the grief, an impossible feat. I'm left with a sense of responsibility toward the sympathizer that renders my burden heavier and heavier.

I left before daybreak to avoid facing Jim and Sylvie again.

When I replayed the conversation in my head the next morning, my laughter burbled and caught, gathered force. I laughed until tears appeared on my face, then I cried for the marriage that hadn't lasted until death parted us.

Road Trip Rule # 62:

Take lots of photos.

# Wayside Ahead:
# Self Defense Class

Women move through the world differently when we're alone than men do. We automatically monitor our surroundings, take note of perceived threats, and formulate exit or avoidance strategies as needed. We stand tall, project confidence, and stride with purpose.

But all the while, we are aware of our own physical vulnerability. We know we might be unable to defend ourselves from an attacker.

We are prey.

When I traveled with Jason, few people said more than hello as we set up at camp sites or went sightseeing. I maintained a vague awareness of others, but I didn't worry about my safety—that was Jason's department.

Alone, women seem approachable. Men frequently trespass on my camp site, ask personal questions, and offer unsolicited, irrelevant advice. Their deliveries range from casual to creepy. I respond in a firm tone, like that of a teacher dealing with a recalcitrant pupil. I do not reveal my unease. I quell my fear.

So far, this has been enough to discourage would-be attackers, assuming I've even encountered any.

Most men act out of curiosity or even some sense

of guardianship when they approach a woman—they're not pernicious. Except for the ones who are.

I took a self-defense class that began, as so many group activities do, with a round of introductions. The trainer, a former policeman named Dean, stood over six feet tall, had broad shoulders and an athletic build.

He played a movie showing a woman jogging on a forest path. A man lurked in the shadows, and jumped out to surprise and attack her as she passed by. Dean paused the movie.

"Ladies, what would you do if this happened to you right now?"

We all glanced around, silently conferring. A woman named Samantha in the front row spoke up in a calm, self-assured voice.

"I'd try to protect myself." She raised her arms and tucked her face into her elbows.

Everyone nodded in agreement.

"I'd try to escape," said Joni, a motherly-looking woman. She shrugged her shoulders. "I mean, if I was a jogger, I'd be in good enough shape to escape, right?"

Chuckles all around.

"I'd kick him in the crotch." This last was from Lisa, who'd introduced herself as a college freshman attending this class under duress from her parents.

"All good answers," said Dean. "Lisa's correct, or at least very close." He paused long enough to glance around and make split-second eye contact with each of us. "Most women have the instinct to protect themselves, and many times it's impossible. You're weaker, he's stronger, and he's been planning this." He paused again to let us consider the implications of a planned attack. "His adrenaline is already pumping. He's taller. He's faster. He's prepared."

"He's not prepared to be kicked in the crotch," said Lisa. She sounded tough.

Dean waited while we murmured our agreement.

"You're right. He's not prepared to be harmed. And that's what every one of you need to be prepared to do. Harm him. Think about that." Another pause for us to imagine hurting another human being. "You have to shed your basic instinct for self-preservation, for self-protection, and prepare yourself to cause harm."

"So...how do we do that?" Samantha asked.

"I'm going to show you some techniques," said Dean. "But I want you to focus on causing harm any way you can. Don't worry about method. Kick, bite, scratch, gouge, scream."

"What if he covers your mouth so you can't scream?" Samantha again.

"Bite his finger off," said Joni. "My sister's a nurse and she said it's like biting off a carrot."

Dean nodded in agreement. "And if that doesn't work, act crazy."

"Crazy?" A timid question from someone in the back row.

Dean brought his hand down, karate-chop style,

with each word or phrase "Sing. Chant. Yell. Say you have diarrhea, gonorrhea, leprosy, herpes. Piss yourself. Whatever you can think of. He's not going to want to deal with a crazy person—he'll leave you there and run off to find an easier target."

Dean taught us how long we should maintain eye contact with a given person—eight to ten seconds—and sometimes that alone will deter an attacker and send him in a different direction. He taught us how to leverage our weight, wriggle out of common holds, and gouge eyeballs with our thumbs. He reminded us that most attackers will seem benign or friendly at first, to gain a sliver of trust before they turn.

"Be firm, ladies. Be a little rude, even. When you engage with him in a friendly manner, that's the first shoe dropping." He mimed dropping a shoe, and hearing it hit the floor. "When you let your guard down, that's the second shoe. The permission," Dean curled his fingers into air quotes, "he's been waiting for. And then it's game over."

He wrapped up the class with one last bit of advice. "We covered a lot today. But if nothing else, I want you to remember two things when you leave here: Prepare to cause harm." He held up a thick index finger. "And try not to get into unsafe situations in the first place." A second finger joined his first one in a peace sign. "And peace out, Girl Scouts." Then he smiled at us for the first time that day.

I've forgotten most of Dean's techniques and I'm not confident I would have the presence of mind to

locate pressure points on a surprise assailant.
But I'm always ready to act crazy.

Road Trip Rule # 11:

The trip isn't over until you stop talking about it.

MILE
9

## Arriving Home

My sister Jen lives three miles from my house, and I stopped at her place on the way home to show off my new rig. Jen climbed in and admired the kitchen and bathroom while her husband Todd walked around the outside and opened up the generator access panel. The kids, Tucker and Jersey, sat at the dinette table as if preparing to play a game of Crazy

Eights.

"How do you like the generator?" Todd asked.

"I'd like it more if it worked. The technician at the dealership had to stick his hand in there to start it." I showed Todd the small panel the dealer had removed. "He said if I let it run for a while, it would clear itself out and would run fine. But it hasn't started since I shut it off."

"Even when you stick your hand in there?"

I shrugged. "Not doing that."

"I don't know if our local guy will work on a propane generator. Maybe he'll know someone who will work on it. It probably just needs a tune-up." Todd walked around to the sliding door, looking at the van as he went. "It's in good shape, though. No troubles with the engine?"

"None. It's easy to drive and I had no problem keeping up with traffic, even through the mountains. And it gets 22 miles per gallon!"

"That's fantastic," said Jen.

"Jersey wants to live in here," said Tucker.

"I don't want to live here, Tucker. I just want to eat dinner and sleep and drive it to the beach," said Jersey.

I told Jen about my redecorating plans.

"It'll be a whole new van when you're finished with it," she said.

"I called the RV place next to the airport in Kinross this morning," I said. "They'll replace the flooring and bathroom faucet."

"Perfect! That gives you all winter to plan what

you'll do on the walls, make the curtains, and whatever else you dream up by then." Jen laughed.

I stayed for coffee, then drove home to unpack and measure for window treatments.

# LEARNING
# CURVES

Road Trip Rule # 77:

Take the side road.

MILE
10

# Early RVs

RVs were born about three generations before I was. The 1910s brought exciting innovations: the Wright Brothers experienced liftoff, Ford assembly line workers were making $5 per day, and the telephone was brand new technology. That decade also witnessed the sinking of the Titanic, World War One, and the creation of the National Park System. Perhaps the combination of these events—lives cut tragically short even while new recreational facilities were planned and built—contributed to the birth of RV camping, which officially began in 1910 when the first mass-manufactured rigs rolled off the assembly lines.

A sign on one of the display models at the RV/MH Hall of Fame in Elkhart, Indiana, claims the title of oldest travel trailer in the world. It's an elegant 1913 Earl Travel Trailer balanced on two spoked wheels and drawn by a Model T Ford. This mobile abode offers a convertible dinette with a long, narrow table and some cabinets for storage. One enters through double doors at the back, each featuring a screened window with a blind on the inside and an insulated panel buttoned on the outside. Worn, golden wood floors and a lacquered lath ceiling offer a level of luxury surprising for its time, and though there are no kitchen or bathroom facilities on this ancient rig, it's warm and welcoming.

The first motor coach appeared even earlier: in 1910 in Montreal, Quebec, a man named U.H. Dandurand hired a carriage builder to outfit his three-ton Packard truck with living quarters using Dandurand's plans. The result was a vehicle twenty-two feet long that could sleep eleven. It also contained a kitchen, complete with an oil stove, icebox, and running water. It even had a toilet. This motor coach was used until the mid-1920s, when it was parked but continued to serve as a summer cottage.

The first Class B equivalent was unveiled at

Madison Square Garden in 1910: the Pierce-Arrow Touring Landau. This progressive vehicle boasted a chamber pot, a fold-down seat attached to the back of the chauffeur's seat, and a telephone used for communication between the driver and the passengers.

The early floor plans and ingenious cabinet placement, and even the convertible dinettes, seem advanced for their day. Just imagine—the first few RVs were built from hand-drawn plans with a dash of pure math thrown in, and they aren't that different from the floor plans and ingenious cabinet placement we find in today's rigs, designed on computers. Some of yesteryear's wood-framed trailers seem more substantial than the current Fiberglas ones.

The new method of camping in a hard-sided tow-behind structure was widely referred to as trailering. The sightseers were referred to as trailerites, or trailerists, or even tin can tourists, a breed of travelers so advanced they easily carried and neatly stowed all the comforts of home while on the road. In 1920 the Tin Can Tourist Association was formed—the first camping group to offer camping events and tips to their members.

Milo Miller, a traveling salesman from Elkhart, Indiana, wanted to take his family with him on the road while he worked. In 1931, he fabricated a small travel trailer using plywood and junked auto parts to tow behind his car. His trailer featured cooking facilities and a wood stove for heat as well as sleeping quarters and the familiar convertible dinette. He sold that trailer to a passerby on his first trip out, then built and sold a second one, and began to manufacture travel trailers full-time.

Miller's trailers were featured at the 1933 Chicago Exposition, where Wilbur Schult happened upon him. Schult bought Miller's company in 1936, changed the name to Schult Homes, and built it into the largest trailer manufacturer in the world. Schult Homes still builds manufactured houses today in Elkhart.

If you're so inclined, stop by the RV/MH Hall of Fame and wander through the vintage RVs on display there. There's an early Schult trailer, the 1939 Nomad, featuring a dapper gray exterior with a slightly rounded nose, a heavy exterior door and a sturdy wooden screen door, and a radio antenna mounted on an outside corner. It's connected to the small radio inset into the counter next to the spacious closet at the front of the rig. They also have Mae West's housecar on display, with its plush driver's seat and inviting back porch. Charles Lindberg's travel trailer is parked directly behind it.

I purchased Donald F. Wood's book, *RVs and Campers 1900-2000: An Illustrated History*, at the RV/MH Hall of Fame gift shop to learn more about the early rigs. One of my favorites was a traveling chapel, circa World War One. This "automobungalow" provided living quarters for the priest, an altar that folded down on the back end, and a private room for confessionals.

There's also mention of a mobile communication device on a 1917 Packard bus that was converted into a motor coach. The driver could simply park next to a utility pole, connect to the telegraph line, and send a message. Easier than a carrier pigeon, quicker than pony express, and no worries about losing cell signal.

The polished wood shells and hardwood floors of those early rigs have been replaced with Fiberglas and laminate to reduce overall weight. Chamber pots have been replaced with fully plumbed bathrooms. The contours have been streamlined to reduce wind resistance. Standard contemporary luxuries now include air conditioning, television, and automatic awnings and jacks.

But the wanderlust is still the same.

Road Trip Rule # 51:

It's never too late to turn around and start over.

## Travel Planning

By the time I winterized the Jan Van and stowed it in my sister's garage for the season, Steph had moved to Alaska to live near Dani. This would be the first Christmas without Mom, without Jason, and without my girls. Instead of dwelling on the losses, I chose to focus on Jen's family and be grateful we lived so close to each other.

I also focused on the van. The renovation became a form of therapy: I'd had the carpeting replaced with laminate flooring; I'd had hoods installed over the ceiling vents so they could remain open during rain showers; and I'd had the bathroom faucet replaced. It was like an age reversal process—each update brought the van a tiny step closer to contemporary. The Jan Van was living backwards right along with me.

When I purchased the van, Joel gave me only one key. This didn't worry me too much until someone pointed out that if I lost the key on one of my road trips, it could cause a delay. The van had a Mercedes diesel engine, a Dodge Sprinter body, and the steering wheel displayed the Freightliner emblem. It had been manufactured during the Mercedes-Dodge partnership, which had since dissolved and left the two companies on less than civil terms. I contacted my local Dodge dealer and discovered they could sell me a blank key, but they couldn't program it—for that, I'd need to visit a Mercedes or Freightliner dealership.

"I'm traveling to Prince Edward Island next month —is this something I could do along the way?" I was standing at the service desk at the Dodge dealership, holding my new, un-programmed van key. It was a Mercedes key that folded into itself, and swung out like a switchblade at the push of a button. The other two buttons on the key locked and unlocked the front doors, but this feature still wasn't working.

The clerk pulled up Google Maps on her computer.

"Show me your route," she said. "I'll find a dealership for you."

She gave me the name and address of a Freightliner dealership north of Burlington, Vermont.

"It'll take them twenty or thirty minutes to program the key," she said.

I added the dealership to my itinerary and paid for my new blank key. It was $250. The Vermont dealership would charge me for the programming.

Meanwhile, I'd discovered there are very few mechanics who will work on propane generators. I scheduled the repair in the spring with a small business in Gaylord, Michigan, about two hours from home. They had to remove the generator to replace the critical component—a process that took two weeks and cost over $800—and then re-install the generator in its side bin. I was now able to start the generator with the remote button inside. I could heat up leftovers in the microwave or blow dry my hair or run the air conditioner. And I didn't have to stick my hand into an engine to do it.

That June, I received notice of a non-critical, voluntary recall to update the Engine Control Unit software on the van. The notice listed a few dealerships in Michigan that could handle it, so I planned to contact one of them after my Prince Edward Island (PEI) trip. It looked like my summer trips would be routed around dealership locations.

My travel goals included using the van at least three out of every four weekends during the summer (which I defined as the months without snow, usually April-October) and logging at least 10,000 miles on it each year. That first spring, I cleaned and stocked the van as soon as the weather permitted and took it camping around the UP and into the northern lower peninsula. I went places I'd never been, and places I hadn't visited in years. Sometimes I met friends and stayed in one campsite for the entire weekend, and sometimes I traveled around at whim on my own. I'd purchased a folding bike for auxiliary transportation —a Citizen-brand neon pink frame with a basket on the front and white-walled tires—it rode shotgun, strapped into the passenger seat in its storage bag.

By the time the calendar flipped to July, I felt comfortable with the van and ready for my first extended trip: seventeen days to drive to PEI and back. Six pages of my bullet journal were dedicated to this trip. I'd made lists of campgrounds, waterfalls, gardens, bookstores, museums, tours, scenic drives, and hiking trails.

I thought I'd planned for everything.

# Quebec To Vermont To Maine

I'd first dreamed of visiting PEI in 1980, when Mom introduced me to *Anne of Green Gables*. Mom read aloud every night when she tucked me into bed, and as I grew older she selected longer and longer books. We progressed through a bookcaseful over those years: *Pippi Longstocking*, *Heidi*, and the entire boxed set of Laura Ingalls Wilder's *Little House* books. *Anne of Green Gables* was the last book she read to me

—I was ten years old by then, and fancied myself too old for bedtime stories. Her reading was far superior to mine, however, and if I'd read those books silently to myself I probably wouldn't remember them so well. I can still hear her voice as she spoke in Matthew Cuthbert's slow cadence. Anne's dialogue and inner thoughts were delivered with a girlish enthusiasm, and Marilla always sounded stern.

In between readings, we held an ongoing discussion about Anne's adventures. PEI sounded almost magical when Anne described it, and Mom and I both yearned to visit Lovers' Lane, the Haunted Wood, and the other places Anne christened in the story.

At ten, I already considered myself a writer. I'd written several volumes of poetry and one short story illustrated with stick figures and bound with staples. Mom, in her role as my biggest fan, encouraged me to keep writing. One of her tactics was to share trivia about the authors who had invented our favorite characters.

"L.M. stands for Lucy Maud," she said once. "But her friends called her Maud. And she also wrote poems. Maud had two imaginary friends when she was a girl."

"I think I'd call myself Lucy." I wrinkled my nose. "Not Maud."

"Who knows," she said. "Maybe you'll be the next L.M. Montgomery."

My imagination felt pale and weak when I

compared it to Maud's. How could I ever hope to develop a character as captivating as Anne? L.M. Montgomery became one of my literary heroes. Mom and I never really stopped talking about Anne Shirley or L.M. Montgomery—their names popped into our conversations as if we'd once known them, as if they were old friends with whom we'd shared tender moments and raucous adventures. In a way, I suppose they were.

Now, I hoped Mom was somehow accompanying me.

I downloaded the entire Anne series of audiobooks so I could listen to them en route and properly set the tone for my adventure.

My itinerary began with a simple plan to drive across Canada and loop back through New England, but it quickly grew to an unrealistic, overly ambitious schedule. An overnight near Montreal, Quebec, a couple of days in Burlington, Vermont, a lovely drive through the scenic Green Mountains, and a stop in St. John, New Brunswick to see the Reversing Falls. (How could an itinerary *not* include a stop at such an intriguing spot?) I added Bar Harbor and Portland, Maine, and two nights near Boston, which warranted its own hour-by-hour plan. I envisioned myself sprinting through the city like the white rabbit in Wonderland, muttering about being late.

The day before I'd planned to leave my excitement level was high. I shifted my work schedule so I could leave that afternoon and reduce the first day's driving time from twelve hours to a manageable eight. I spent the night in Mattawa, Ontario, at a four-star campground that featured a weak WiFi signal near the office and a lovely view of the Mattawa River. The mosquitoes were well-organized and hungry, and the sunset a vivid blend of pink and orange reflected on the river.

However, I quickly realized I'd skimped on Montreal research. I'd known I wouldn't have cell signal, but I'd failed to consider how that would impact my on-the-go research, which was to eliminate it completely. I'd written down the address of the Montreal Botanical Gardens, and I made my way downtown to the proper parking lot without incident. If you've ever driven in Montreal, you'll realize this was a major victory. I have no idea what the local architecture looks like, as I had to keep my eyes trained on the traffic. It seemed as if all four million citizens were racing around the city, each in their own car.

The gardens were worth the trip, though. They're much larger than I'd expected, and feature several different botanical themes: a rose garden, a shade garden, a Japanese garden, a natural sculpture garden. They're linked by paths, some of which wind beneath leafy canopies and around ponds. Even with a map, it was easy to get disoriented and visit the same garden twice. I unfolded my travel bike and cruised along the bike path after wandering through the gardens. The city noises receded to a low-level hum within the park.

I left Montreal after a mid-morning snack in the Jan Van, and set off toward the Vermont border.

Some people collect trinkets while on vacation. They return home with tchotchke from every destination they visit, be it Disney World or Rome. Shot glasses, wine bottle stoppers, refrigerator magnets, pillows. Some buy t-shirts or tote bags or key chains. I fall prey to these purchases sometimes, too—there are sweatshirts and magnets and a keychain or three from my travels tucked into my closet and car.

But the thing I seek out while roaming the globe, the thing I buy on purpose, is a vacation talisman. A good luck charm found somewhere along my route that will protect me from calamities and mishaps. The search is entertaining and I end up with something to help me remember the trip. I never know what I'm looking for until I find it.

On this trip, I found my talisman just in time—mere hours before I needed some positive energy.

I stopped in St. Albans, Vermont, and spent a few hours shopping and walking. I bought a bracelet of fluorite beads which, according to the store clerk, offers protection, increases intellect, and cleanses the aura of those who wear it. I'm not sure any of this is true, but it's fun just the same. I had my talisman.

The blank van key would be programmed at a Freightliner dealer in Milton, about twenty minutes north of Burlington. I arrived at my appointment early, expecting the programming to take about thirty minutes, as stated when I'd made the appointment a few weeks before the trip.

Two hours later, the mechanic informed me he'd tried to replace a recalled software module, and it hadn't worked. Now my check engine light was on and there was a high probability the van would stop running with little or no warning. I would have to stick around until Monday, when they would receive the overnight shipment of another replacement module.

"I'm not here for a recall."

"It's printed on the ticket." He showed me the work order with the recall information circled in red.

"Isn't this a voluntary recall?" I asked. "I didn't volunteer to fix this here. I have an appointment with another dealer in Michigan, after my trip."

"It's voluntary until you go to a dealer. We can't release a vehicle with an unaddressed recall. I'm sorry."

"What? No. I made the appointment to program the key. I was told it would take thirty minutes."

"Like I said, we don't have a choice. I'm sorry." He held out my receipt and I snatched it from his greasy hand.

"Why do you have more authority over my vehicle than I do?" My breath hitched in my chest and my voice climbed an octave.

He mumbled another apology and summoned Chet, who fit me into a morning slot on Monday's schedule. I asked Chet why this wasn't mentioned to me when I made the appointment but he only shrugged and claimed ignorance.

"At least change your policy," I said.

"What do you mean?"

"At least, from now on, tell people when there's a recall you have to address when they make the appointment. I don't mind pausing for a half hour to program a key, but I wouldn't have agreed to staring at your waiting room walls for several hours during my vacation. This is absurd."

"Look, I'm sorry. I don't know who you talked to, and I don't know who noticed the recall. I really wish it had worked out and you were back on the road. We'll do our best on Monday morning. And if you need a tow between now and then, we won't charge you for it."

I tried not be sullen. It wasn't the mechanic's fault, it wasn't Chet's fault, it wasn't my fault. There was nobody to blame, which was the most frustrating part of the situation.

By the time I left the dealership it was Friday afternoon and I'd wasted several precious vacation hours. I'd planned to head east before sunrise on Sunday morning and meander through New Hampshire to Maine with plenty of time to visit waterfalls and hike a few trails. This repair would delay my departure until Monday at the earliest. Dejected and dispirited, I found a cafe in Burlington and treated myself to lunch with a glass of wine (and whine).

I ran the fluorite bracelet through my fingers, reminding myself to stay buoyant. I began to view the delay as a gift of time. I pulled out my itinerary and crossed Bar Harbor off the schedule, rationalizing that I really hadn't allowed enough time to properly explore all of Acadia anyway. It would've been packed with other tourists, the traffic would have slowed me down, and I wouldn't have seen everything I'd planned, which was pretty much everything listed on the brochures I'd received months before. Also, I'd never been to Burlington before, so this provided an opportunity to stay an additional day and a half. This attitude gave me a little buzz: spontaneity had knocked on my door, and I ushered her in. As someone who plans every detail from embarkation to homecoming, and all points in between, spontaneity has always remained aloof. She is the guest I wished would attend my party even though I feel ill-equipped to mingle with her. Yet here I was, offering her a chair and reviewing my list of auxiliary itinerary items for Burlington. The talisman tinkled as I shifted the van into gear.

I'd reserved a site at the North Beach Campground for Friday night because of its easy access to the bike path that follows the lakeshore to the city center. The campground is a city-owned facility, and it features 137 campsites on its 45 acres. Mine was a narrow slot between two other campers, with barely enough room to wedge the van next to the picnic table. The fire ring was under water at the back of the site. The campground receptionist at the front desk had mentioned recent torrential rains, and there were telltale puddles throughout the park.

On one side of my campsite, a tablecloth printed with gigantic pink and orange flowers was draped over a chair. When the tablecloth moved I realized it was a muumuu, covering the largest woman I'd ever seen. The muumuu featured wide horizontal stripes of sweat. She sat quashed into a reinforced anti-gravity chair next to an oddly permanent-looking chainlink fence containing three large German shepherds. The fenced area was about eight feet square—the dogs practiced synchronized pacing to avoid bumping into each other. The woman turned her head to yell at the dogs, then turned her head to yell at her husband for spending money on his stupid Mustang when he knew damn well she wanted new carpeting. The dogs and the husband ignored her. I was riveted.

My other neighbor was a hairless man in shorts and flip flops. His wife bustled around inside their fifth wheel while he sat, legs crossed and wine glass in hand, in a screen tent beneath the gooseneck of his trailer. He looked like a member of the witness protection program: an indistinct silhouette camouflaged by the screen.

"You should've parked at an angle." His voice purred from the shadows. "You'd have more room if you parked at an angle." The wine glass moved to his featureless face. His right foot bobbed up and down, the sandal hanging on one toe. I waved his words aside on my way to retrieve the electric cord.

Parking at an angle made no sense here; it was a long, narrow site and the electric outlet was near the back. I plugged in the electric cord, stepped inside, and slid the van door shut.

Early the following morning, I woke to a light rain and abandoned my bike-riding plan. The forecast promised intermittent showers all day Saturday and into Sunday—at this rate, the campground might never dry up. I filled my fresh water tank and dumped my black and gray tanks. If the van broke down, I'd be prepared to stay a night or two in the mechanic's lot. I left the campground before any of the neighbors emerged from their campers, and found a convenient parking space downtown. The space nearly fit the entire van. I parked with the front wheels on one line and the back wheels on one line, and hoped the city would grant me a few inches of leeway for my bumpers.

I started my exploration of Burlington—Vermont's Queen City—at the farmers' market, where I chatted with the young man selling small batch Vermont Hummus, the woman who baked twelve kinds of bread, and various gardeners and jewelry makers. When the rain let up, a woman staged herself near the fountain and played show tunes on her accordion, the open case near her feet filling fast with cash. A Siberian husky waded in the fountain and lapped the water. The park looked like an episode of Gilmore Girls sprung to life, with wandering Burlingtoners greeting each other and enjoying a slow Saturday morning.

Next, I toured the Church Street Marketplace, a three-block pedestrian through-way with a brick surface lined with boutiques, bookstores, and restaurants. In front of the yoga studio, twenty-two people on jewel-toned mats in neat rows greeted the sun. A scruffy, gray-haired man in tattered clothes asked me for a quarter as he staggered along the sidewalk. I handed him the dollar I'd received in change from the hummus table.

The Crow Bookshop looks like the neighborhood bookstore we should all remember from our childhoods. Books crowded floor-to-ceiling shelves, a literary bulwark protecting patrons from despair and unease. I browsed the sale table in the middle of the floor while the wall of books stood sentry behind me.

I returned to the van with my hummus, bread, and bagful of books and ate lunch on a bench in the park perched on the edge of Lake Champlain. The clouds had moved on, leaving me with a blue sky and warm breeze off the lake. I walked a loop around the park with the joggers, wanderers, and dog walkers who seemed happy to share this meteorological bounty.

After my walk, I consulted my list of alternate Burlington sites, chose one, and programmed the address of a vintage store into my GPS.

What a find! It's near the world's tallest filing

cabinet, which warranted a brief stop for a photo along the way.

The clerk at Deep Six was the owner's father. His son had purchased the store a couple of years before, and he went on annual buying trips to the Boston area with a semi truck and trailer, returning with enough merchandise to stock up for the year. I found a 1940s melamine appetizer tray with a simple branch and flower pattern and set it on the counter.

"Are you familiar with the term Deep Six?" He asked.

"Doesn't it mean to bury something, or throw it away?"

"Yep! It used to mean burial at sea, six fathoms deep, but then everyone started saying it whenever they wanted something to disappear. As in, deep six it."

"You've saved all of these things from being deep-sixed." I gestured at the wares with a wave of my arm.

"He finds the damnedest things," said the clerk. "He has an eye for it. Like that, over there." He pointed to a portable record player with Howdy Doody's upside down face grinning from the open cover. A sold sticker dangled from the handle.

"Why in the world anyone would buy that is beyond me." He chuckled. "But I'm glad they do. I'm retired, so me and the wife help him out as much as we can."

We chatted a while longer and he directed me to another vintage thrift store. I drove by it, but it had already closed for the weekend. A glass blowing studio beckoned from across the street, though, so I stopped there and joined the other tourists lined up at the railing separating the working studio from the observation area. The graceful movements of the glass blowers as they heated the glass rods in the fiery furnace mesmerized us.

I wouldn't last an entire day at work if random strangers observed my every move and I said as much to the woman standing next to me. We were so close, I was in her perfume bubble.

"Honey, I wouldn't last five minutes." She pulled out a tube of orangey-red lipstick and applied another coat to her already vibrant lips. She patted my arm and walked outside on pink stilettos, her tropical-patterned capris catching the sun as she emerged from the dark studio.

I wandered outside and returned to the van. The sun had lost its heat, and I was hungry. Evening was descending fast. I drove to the shopping complex south of town, where they allowed RVs to park for free overnight. There were three others already parked in the far corner of the lot, and I parked nearby as the sun was setting.

The protocol for staying in store parking lots overnight is simple: don't set up anything outside, don't run the generator for more than a few minutes, and don't disturb anyone. Basically, it's a free parking spot—not a free campsite. I locked the van and closed my curtains so no one would realize I was traveling alone, and relaxed with a book and a glass of wine before turning in for the night.

Sunday delivered as promised by the weather forecast. The clouds were low, the wind chilly, the rain the kind that soaks through everything quickly and thoroughly.

I spent the day shopping and driving around Burlington's outskirts. The rain persisted all day, so I went to my campsite just before dinner.

I'd found a campground near Milton, closer to the dealership for my appointment the following morning. The Maple Grove Campground offered level sites and room enough to enjoy a bonfire without risking melting the neighbors' camper— already an upgrade from the micro-site between the muumuu and the whisperer. I bought a bundle of firewood and built a fire. The rain had diminished to a drizzle, so I opened my awning and ate outside while the fire crackled.

Three men slowly walked by, and one stepped onto my site while the other two waited on the road.

"Excuse me," he said. "We have a question." He looked about fifty, with a balding head and a large belly draped in a Hawaiian print. The two friends he'd left on the road were tall and lean with matching gray goatees and blue polo shirts.

"Sure," I said.

"We were wondering—what's the round thing on your roof?"

"It's a TV antenna. I don't have a TV inside, but

the previous owners had one installed."

"Huh. So, you're traveling alone?"

The real question revealed itself. His friends had been joking about a woodpecker knocking on a tree, but they stopped talking and seemed to be waiting for my answer.

"Somewhat. I'm meeting friends along the way." I tried to sound confident. Strong. Unflappable.

He smiled, then rocked back on his heels and glanced at his buddies, who nodded. "Good for you." He waved and they resumed their campground tour. I listened to them circle around and return to their site, just down the hill from mine.

I burned through my slim bundle of firewood without further interruption, one eye out for the three curious men. I didn't see them again.

The next morning, I twisted a quarter into the shower timer for five minutes of hot, miserly water flow. It wouldn't accept a second quarter, so I scrubbed hard and fast. The water ran out before I washed my face—I had to subject myself to the glacial trickle in the sink. At least using the campground shower had saved me the bother of refilling my fresh water tank before pulling out of the campground.

My check engine light had remained on all weekend, but the van seemed to be running alright. It was impossible to know whether I was wasting my time with this repair or not. They'd promised an early morning time slot and said I'd be on the road by noon at the latest. I took a circuitous route through Fairfax to the dealership and arrived twenty minutes before they opened. Several employees were already bustling about, and Chet, the clerk I'd met earlier, told me as soon as they received the part in the morning mail delivery, they'd move me to the top of the docket.

"You'll be out of here by 10:00 AM," he said.

While I waited for the part to be delivered I consulted my map and programmed various destinations into my phone. The campground I'd planned to visit in St. John, New Brunswick, was eight and a half hours away, assuming there was no traffic, perfect weather, and zero stops. I crossed off sights I'd planned to see along the way—the goal now was pure progress. Not an ideal road-tripping circumstance.

The part was delivered at 9:15, and they began work on the van at 9:25. Once again, I waited on a vinyl chair in the lobby while the clock on the wall ticked on and on. Chet occasionally threw a compassionate glance my way and said, "They're working on it."

At 12:30, I asked if I could access the van to grab something to eat.

"Of course! It's your vehicle."

"Is it?" *If it's my vehicle*, I thought, *I should be authorized to refuse a voluntary recall.*

Chet laughed. I let him think I was kidding.

I tamped down my frustration and walked into the garage, startling the two men standing near the van.

"We're working on it," the tall one said. He had a black mustache and a faded red mis-buttoned shirt.

"So I've heard," I grumbled.

"We had to reprogram every injector," said the bowlegged one. "And then the check engine light came back on." He shrugged and walked toward the back of the shop. His work boots were worn down on the outsides of his soles. A chewing tobacco streak ran down the center of his beard.

"Do you know how much longer it might be?" I asked the one with the mustache.

"We have a call into Mercedes right now. We're hoping we just missed a reset button or something minor." He caressed his mustache with greasy fingers. "These babies are sometimes more complicated than they appear."

I ate in the van while I pored over the atlas. There was no way I'd make St. John at this rate. I emailed the St. John campground and let them know I wouldn't make it. They replied immediately and said they hoped to meet me in the future sometime. No harm, no foul.

After a brisk two laps around the entire parking lot, I returned to the waiting room. One other woman was there who'd been stranded on the road. Her husband arrived to pick her up. They said the repair to her car would take at least a week.

I silently thanked the universe for repairing my van faster than that.

Finally, at 2:43 PM, Chet informed me the van was

finished and I was all set.

"They finally got the check engine light to go out. Call us if you have any problems."

I zoomed away before they could change their minds, and drove for about twenty minutes before I encountered the first uphill climb. The check engine light came on and the van sputtered until I let up on the pedal, then regained its verve at the crest of the hill. When I called the shop, Chet said it had nothing to do with the repairs they'd just done. He said this as if he expected me to believe him.

"I drove this van through the Blue Ridge and the Smokies, and never had a problem," I said. "It has never sputtered before. That's a brand new development, since the visit to your shop."

"Maybe you're driving faster than you were in the Smokies. Or maybe it's a steeper hill. There are too many variables for me to provide an answer. But if the engine light is back on, you should call Freightliner."

My mind swirled with indecision. The Green Mountains might prove impassable. Should I continue on as planned, and hope I didn't break down? Or should I turn toward home and sacrifice my entire trip? Or should I find another Freightliner dealership or shop and see if they could fix what might now be two unrelated problems?

The van continued to purr along, except on steep upgrades. It no longer downshifted as needed to propel itself up and over hills and mountains. I thought again about the mountains I'd zoomed over on my way home from Florida the previous year. There'd been no sign of flagging power, no sputtering, no hesitation. This was like driving an entirely different vehicle.

The Freightliner representative said he couldn't advise me to continue driving the van with the check engine light on, and the nearest Freightliner dealership along my path was located in Bangor, Maine. They wouldn't be open the following day, because it was the Fourth of July.

I continued driving east on US-2 while I mulled over my predicament, winding around mountains and alongside streams, meeting the occasional car or pickup truck. It was a peaceful drive except for the chatter inside my head.

I drove past a sign announcing the way to Screw Auger Falls. My original plan for the drive from Vermont to Maine had included several stops at waterfalls, and I recognized the name of this one. It was about nine miles from US-2 on Highway 26, also known as Bear River Road. I needed to stop and stretch. I needed to walk around and eat something. I hated the thought of tacking twenty additional minutes of driving time to my day, but after so many itinerary cancelations, I craved the sight of a waterfall from my original plan.

I paused and stuffed five dollars into the donation box as I entered the parking area. My body had grown tense while driving and mulling—my shoulders felt like the petrified wood I remembered from a childhood trip to South Dakota. Screw Auger Falls consist of a few cascades and a plunge, and they begin a few steps from the parking area. I exchanged my sandals for a more sturdy pair of shoes and locked the van.

Well-worn granite extended to the water's edge, where several people dangled their feet in the water. A few were wading, and one woman in a pink swimsuit sat on a rock ledge that provided a natural shower area adjacent to a twelve-foot cascade. This wasn't the main plunge—I found that farther up the trail in a naturally sculpted gorge. I shot a couple of photos of the twenty-five-foot plunge with my phone to document my visit, but the view deserved my good camera. Hyperaware of the time passing, I nevertheless took a moment to stand on the rock and behold the waterfall. The water masked the sound of the swimmers; no traffic noises blemished the experience. It was an oasis out of the stress of the day.

I stood there another five minutes, then returned to the van and assembled a bowl of grapes, chunks of cheese, and crackers. A snack dinner for the road.

The minute I turned east on US-2, my mind snapped back to its obsessive mulling. If I took the van to Bangor, I'd have to stay there until at least July fifth, when they'd reopen. I may have to wait for parts, or for their mechanics to have time to fit me in. The sun was dropping to the tree line when I finally decided to drive as far as Bangor and reassess. So far, nothing else had changed. All of the gauges on the dashboard were within their regular ranges and by anticipating the sputtering and letting up on the pedal, the only difference was a longer, slower climb up each hill.

I explained all of this to my sister on a hurried phone call, and told her I'd text her when I'd settled for the night.

I passed several unmarked parking spots along the highway and in the small towns that dotted the area. Most likely, nobody would've noticed or cared if I'd parked in one of those for the night, but I was afraid I'd be rudely awakened by the police in the wee hours if I took the chance. A quick consultation of the camping app on my phone revealed nearby Mount Blue State Park. The online listing promised WiFi and electric hook-ups, and a quick phone call verified they had vacancy. Perfect.

The GPS said I'd arrive in five minutes.

I turned north onto Highway 156, and continued on until the GPS directed me to turn right. The State Park road sign indicated the picnic grounds were on the right, but the campground was straight ahead. I ignored the GPS and continued straight another few miles, then turned left as indicated by another sign. I encountered one or two more signs along the way, dim promises in the diminishing daylight of a campground up ahead. I shut the GPS off to stop its incessant recalculating. I'd lost cell signal when I passed the picnic area, and I was now twenty minutes from US-2. The road wound illogically through an ominous forest, around a pond, past a field, and up a mountain until I expected to return to the highway at a point I'd already traveled.

Finally, at the pinnacle of what must have been Mount Blue, my headlights revealed the check-in station. I left the van running and jogged over to the cabin.

The clerk's nameplate said Daisy, and she looked like the Daisy character on Downton Abbey, right down to the white apron she wore over her blouse.

"I'm the one who called you a few minutes ago for a site, for tonight only." I sounded a bit brusque, and smiled to soften my tone—it wasn't Daisy's fault I'd let a subpar mechanic throw a wrench into my trip. "It's been a long day."

"You just made it! I was about to lock the gate for the night. Here's a map of the campground." She spun a map around so I could view it. Most of the sites were highlighted in green or yellow. "The ones that aren't highlighted are available."

"Which ones have electric service?"

She shook her head, eyes wide. "Oh, we don't have electric service here at all. This station is run on solar power."

"So—no WiFi either, then. The website says you have both electric and WiFi."

"People keep telling me that." She shrugged. "No, none of that here. We are quite rustic."

By now the sky was dark and I was at least thirty minutes from the nearest town, and even farther from the next closest campground. I hadn't texted my sister, and now I wouldn't be able to until the following day. The mere thought of driving back to US-2 was enough to make me cry, and if there was a silver lining, I couldn't see it. This was beyond the powers of the talisman.

"I'll take site number six." I pointed to the map.

I drove around to site number six and backed in. It was a narrow site with dense evergreen walls. I turned off the fridge, crawled into bed, and slept hard until 5:00 AM. It was still dark when I pulled out of the park fifteen minutes later, hoping for a day with no canceled plans.

I imagine Mount Blue State Park offers spectacular views, perhaps a few interesting hiking trails, maybe a waterfall...who knows? Certainly not me.

Road Trip Rule # 46:

Never miss a sunrise.

MILE
1
3

# Prince Edward Island

The next morning crept in, silent and foggy. A young moose nosed his way out of the swampy area along the low straightaway at the bottom of Mount Blue. I stopped on the road and shot photos of him watching me in the morning gloom.

When I entered the land of cell signal and coffee shops, I bought a cup of coffee and left a review for the Mount Blue State Park Campground on the camping app that praised the staff and the lovely sites, but warned about the lack of amenities. I also texted my sister, who was glad to learn I'd survived the night.

The check engine light continued to taunt me from the dashboard and the odometer light flickered on every once in a while. The engine seemed to struggle and lose power from 45 to 55 miles per hour, then it recovered and glided on.

I decided to press on. I'd waited far too long and I'd driven far too many miles to turn back now. At worst, I was risking a breakdown in a rural area that might cost obscene amounts of time and money. At best, the van would continue running without further incident and I'd get to see Prince Edward Island.

The towns I drove through bustled with Fourth of July preparations. Bunting and banners abounded, and crepe-paper-bedecked cars, trucks, and tractors crept along the streets. People set up chairs along the sidewalks in a couple of the towns, and kids ran around like fireflies, energetic and aimless. In one small village, an Uncle Sam on stilts walked alongside the firetruck. They were the same height.

According to Google Maps, I was within a block of Stephen King's house when I cruised through his hometown of Bangor, Maine. I craned my neck and strained my eyes but no dark-haired men wearing glasses and thoughtful expressions were trudging along the sidewalk.

I continued on, stopping only for fuel before crossing the border into Canada.

I'd originally planned to spend a night in St. John, New Brunswick, before entering Prince Edward Island. St. John is the home of the Reversing Falls and a quaint downtown area, which looked easy to bicycle when I checked the map online. Although the dealership's delay had caused me to cancel my night in St. John, I still wanted to see the Reversing Falls, a portion of the St. John River that actually reverses its flow twice a day when the tide comes in.

My timing was nearly perfect—I caught the last few moments of the reversal, when the water was swirling madly and looked as if it would swallow anything that dropped into its vortex. There's a visitors' center there, and a couple of viewing platforms, all of which made for a nice leg stretcher. It was sunny and cool, and I made lunch in the van and ate at one of the picnic tables sprinkled about the little park.

When the Reversing Falls isn't reversing, it's a regular river flowing into the ocean. Nothing much to see. I packed up and drove on, and crossed Confederation Bridge around 4:00 PM.

Before 1997, the only access to PEI with a vehicle was by ferry boat, which didn't operate during the winter months when ice locked out the Island from the rest of the world. Confederation Bridge is two lanes wide, eight miles long and appears, in the beginning, to have no end. The toll is charged by the round-trip as people exit the Island. If I wanted to save forty-six Canadian dollars, I could simply remain on the Island. I considered this option several times during my visit.

The first thing I saw on PEI was a statue of Anne Shirley, from *Anne of Green Gables*, waving hello. She looked like I'd always envisioned: sun hat, friendly grin, braids, dress, and a basket of flowers on one arm. The visitors' center is behind her, and a couple of blocks of tourist shops are lined up behind the center. I grabbed some information from the visitors' center, then walked to the end of the boardwalk. Sun sparkled on the water and the ocean smelled salty and fresh, at high tide.

I drove toward Charlottetown and the KOA campground where I'd booked my site for the next six nights. I felt like I was driving through a painting. Vibrant purple lupine bordered the farm fields, deep red earth dotted with orderly rows of emerald green potato plants, and the rolling hills and old barns looked like real life art. The traffic was light, and I easily found the campground and backed into my assigned site.

Each site was about twelve feet wide. I had full hook-ups, but my short drain hose wouldn't reach the sewer pipe lid when I was hooked up to the water and electric. I ate a quick dinner and walked around the campground—all six hundred sites—and discovered the red sand beach, the back field, and all of the microscopic-sized sites in between.

The campground was nearly at capacity—I counted eight empty spaces—and campers were hanging out, cooking dinner, sitting around campfires, watching the kids run and bike around the narrow lanes.

When I returned to the van, my camping neighbors greeted me and waved me over. They looked relaxed and friendly, and I could hear two girls giggling in their camper. I introduced myself to Mike and Christie from Sarnia, Ontario. They both worked at a prison.

"A Canadian prison?" I asked. "Is it like a time-out chair in the corner, or do you lock up jaywalkers and people who run stop signs?"

Christie laughed. "No, we actually have real criminals over here."

"Nothing like in the States, of course," said Mike.

"They're probably all from the States," I said.

Christie giggled again. "That's what we always say."

"So, you're alone, aren't you?" Mike asked.

My least favorite question.

"Yep. I'm from Michigan—the Upper Peninsula—and I've wanted to come to PEI since I read the book, probably like most other people who visit here. I'm a walking literary cliche."

He pointed skyward. "I knew it when you pulled in. I said to Christie, 'she's traveling alone.' I could tell there wasn't anyone else in the van."

"He did," said Christie. "You're brave to do that. Good for you."

"Thanks," I said. "I don't know if it's bravery or stupidity, but so far, so good."

"Well, you can't live life being scared all the time," said Christie. She turned toward the camper and called to her daughters. "Time for your shower!"

"They never want to take a shower," said Mike. "But I know it won't be long and they'll be taking two or three showers per day, so we just hang in there."

"I remember my own transition from grunge to Barbie Doll," said Christie. "My parents hated both of those phases. I eventually pulled out of it."

"Every phase has its challenges," I said. "Even the phase I'm in right now, which seems to be middle-aged solo traveler. I'm challenging myself."

They both laughed.

We were both staying for five days, but their reservation had begun two days before I arrived. I ate a quick dinner and joined them at their campfire, glass of wine in hand.

\*\*\*

My first full day on PEI began with a wire-wrapping class I'd reserved on AirBNB.com. I'd made wire-wrapped jewelry before, but I wanted a piece of PEI beach glass, and I hoped to learn something new at the same time.

The jewelry studio was located in the back room of a house, which also had a tiny gift shop full of— take a guess—wire-wrapped sea glass. I chose a piece of light green sea glass, learned the artist's technique, and handcrafted my own beautiful pendant for fifteen dollars.

After the class, I drove to downtown Charlottetown and parked the van in a spacious seaside parking lot for free. It's placed between a small residential area and the ocean, and is adjacent to Confederation Park, a grassy area with paved sidewalks and flower beds. I meandered through the park for a few minutes before heading down Queen Street.

Colorful gabled Victorian houses lined the streets, and the storefronts beckoned with large, inviting display windows just old-fashioned enough to be inviting without being fusty. I ate lunch on Victoria Row, a street open to pedestrians only, at an outside table in front of a chic little cafe. I'd planned to order lobster, but a spicy rice dish with mussels caught my eye on the menu. It was delicious.

After lunch, I walked over to The Guild to watch the musical Anne & Gilbert, for which I'd purchased a ticket six months earlier. It was a grand performance, and incorporated many of the events in the third Anne of Green Gables book, *Anne of the Island*, which I'd just finished listening to that morning.

The love story acted out on stage, and the couple sitting next to me, who were celebrating fifty years of marriage with this vacation, made me miss Jason like an unbroken promise. I knew he wouldn't have enjoyed the performance, and I knew he wouldn't have enjoyed most of this trip, but I missed him, or the idea of him. We had traveled together for so many years, it was hard to believe I now traveled alone even while I was doing it.

After the performance, I shopped my way back to the van and purchased a short autobiography of Lucy Maud Montgomery called *The Alpine Path: The Story Of My Career*.

I drove back to the campsite and reconnected my electrical cord. Mike and Christie were sitting around their campfire, and chatting with them lifted my spirits some. I drank a glass of wine and went to bed early, my essential oil diffuser pumping out the uplifting scent of lemongrass.

The next morning, I bounded out of bed before the alarm went off and ran over to the shower house. I sprayed the shower with Lysol, and wiped the bench area with a Clorox wipe, which turned brown with dirt. I used two more wipes and wore my sandals in the shower. After all of this effort and preparation, conserving propane by not using the water heater was starting to seem silly—next time, I would shower in the van.

I returned to the van and prepared for the day, ending with pouring a second cup of coffee and setting out for the Jacques Cartier Provincial Park, on the northeast tip of the Island. The rolling hills and verdant potato farms were interspersed with tiny towns, and I arrived at the park invigorated and happy. I walked the beach for a while, taking photos and marveling at the beautiful red sand.

After I'd had my fill of the beach, I climbed back into the van and set off in search of the Bottle Houses, a place I'd found on a travel website months before the trip. The Bottle Houses were created before recycling was widely practiced. Edouard Arsenault began collecting bottles in the 1970s to construct artful, life-sized Bottle Houses, using colorful votives discarded by the Catholic parishes as well as bottles he rescued from the town dump. Before long, people began bringing their bottles to him. He constructed a chapel using 10,000 bottles; a six-gabled house, using 12,000 bottles; and a saloon, complete with a central column, a bar, and dazzling designs embedded in the walls. When word of his project spread, people sent bottles from all over the world. Many of his most unique bottles are sitting on display on the bar in his Bottle Saloon.

The Bottle Houses are set in a beautiful garden with a pond and fountain and, of course, a gift shop. Arsenault's creativity is beautiful to behold, and after wandering the gardens and spending some time in each of his creations, I felt inspired to tackle my own landscaping projects (this feeling would pass by the time I returned home).

From the Bottle Houses, I headed to Summerside to meet the guide for my Segway tour. Jason and I had planned to take a Segway tour in several of the cities we'd visited during our travels, but something always prevented us. The weather, the availability or timing, or the scheduling of other events always caused us to drop the Segway from our plans. When I found the Segway tour website while researching this trip, I was determined to finally do it, and nothing was going to stop me.

I parked down the block from the tour place, ate a quick lunch in the van, then walked around a few blocks before entering the tour headquarters. Greg, my tour guide, had just dropped off his previous clients at their private plane—they'd flown from Ontario for the afternoon so they could tour Summerside on a Segway. I was the only client on the 1:00 tour, but Greg made me feel like he preferred it that way. After watching the safety video and running through a quick training course in which Greg pronounced me "a natural", we set off along the beachside boardwalk.

The Segway, or personal transportation device, was easy to control. I stood with my feet about hip-width apart and gripped the handlebars. Operating it required a subtle weight re-distribution. To move forward, I pressed my toes down and leaned ever so slightly forward—almost as if I merely thought about leaning, but didn't really do it. To stop, I slowly transferred my weight back on my heels. I made turns with the same method, being mindful of Greg's warnings and making large, sweeping turns rather than attempting tight corners.

The Segway tour was easily the highlight of my vacation so far. Greg was a fabulous guide, sharing several interesting facts about Summerside and PEI with me. The most astounding was probably the amount of potatoes produced on PEI. Fully one third of the world's potatoes come from PEI, with the other two thirds coming from Idaho and Russia in fairly equal amounts. Evidently the red earth, the angle of the sun, and the not-too-scant rainfall create the perfect biome in which to grow the world's most popular vegetable.

The Fitzgeralds and Rockefellers visited Summerside in its heyday, staying in a luxury hotel on Holman Island across the bay, and shopping in Holman's, advertised as "the world's biggest small-town department store", located in downtown Summerside. Many ships were produced in Summerside, too, ordered by shipping magnates from the Boston States and as far south as Alabama. During my visit to PEI, I heard several people refer to the New England area as the Boston States, a throwback term from Colonial times.

Our tour continued along the boardwalk to the wharf and the new downtown location of Holland College. There, we turned around and headed to the other end of the boardwalk, built on a former railroad track. We rolled through a marsh, across bridges, past a new residential development and a newly reincarnated resort still under construction, and into a forest where the boardwalk finally ended on the beach with an expansive view of the lighthouse and point. Greg stopped for a moment while I took photos.

"Do you know why the sand is red?" Greg asked as I framed my picture of the lighthouse.

I ventured a weak guess. "From the minerals in the ocean?"

"Close!" Greg grinned. "High iron content in the soil surrounding the Island causes this rusty red color."

It sounded obvious after he said it.

"When the tide goes out, the sand heats up fast, again due to the high iron content, and warms the water when the tide comes back in," Greg explained. "That's why our beaches are the warmest ones north of Florida."

I stopped fiddling with my camera and looked at him. "North of Florida? There are a lot of beaches between here and there."

He nodded. "That's why PEI is so incredible."

Summerside is a town of many surprises, and I'm grateful I took the Segway tour and learned more about it. My mood was up again; I was back in my default happy mode, maybe a notch or two higher than usual because I was on vacation. And not just any vacation, but on PEI! Is there any better situation in the world than when you're on vacation and the weather cooperates and the day consists of one pleasant surprise after another?

The next day was dedicated to L.M. Montgomery, and it began with another beach walk while I waited for the Anne of Green Gables Provincial Park to open. The park is in Cavendish, a seaside village near the midpoint of the northern shore. The beaches are long and the sand is nearly white. The cliffs along the edge of the point, however, are red.

Green Gables was originally Maud's uncle's house, and Maud lived across what is now the highway entering town, with her grandmother, Lucy MacNeill. While Green Gables is still intact and welcomes thousands of tourists each year, the homestead that held many of Maud's childhood memories was destroyed years ago. A peaceful stroll from Green Gables to the MacNeill homestead, via the Haunted Wood, allowed time to soak in the setting. It's rare one can experience a storybook legend brought to life, and I reveled in every second. Plaques placed along the Haunted Wood trail heighten the experience— some display quotes from L.M. Montgomery, some contain explanations about the woods and the bridge over the stream. It's easy to imagine a young Maud finding plenty of inspiration in this beautiful, peaceful setting.

Across the highway, the path continues to the foundation of the old house and a cabin-like bookstore with more memorabilia. I purchased Maud's biography, titled *Lucy Maud Montgomery - The Gift of Wings*, by Mary Henley Rubio, and the clerk happily stamped it with an official stamp indicating it was purchased at the Site of Lucy Maud Montgomery's Cavendish Home, and another stamp of L.M. Montgomery's signature. It's a thick volume, written by the woman who edited all five of Maud's journals.

"This is the best book to buy, unless you want to read all five of her journals," said the clerk as she stamped the book for me.

I left the cabin and continued on to the post office, which Maud's grandmother managed when Maud was a child, and then returned to the original path near the old well. I wondered how many of Maud's wishes had been whispered into the well, but she might just as well have chosen the apple trees or the bubbling brook to receive her wishes, as drawn as she was to trees and water.

I took a moment to wander through the cemetery and locate Maud's grave. She lies at rest with her family, across the highway from her childhood home. I wondered what she'd make of modern-day Cavendish. Would she be surprised and dismayed at the highway that split the town? What would she think of her childhood home being toured by masses of Anne fans? I hoped she would have viewed the tourist sights as a boon for the local economy. A way to allow those who loved the area to live and thrive there.

When I returned to Green Gables, Anne Shirley stood on the front lawn talking to a child. He told her he'd heard about all of her stories.

"I have no idea who would have written such things!" Anne said. She looked around, as if someone might confess. "I'll have to find out who was telling these stories—are they true, these stories?"

"Yes," said the boy. He widened his eyes. "Every single one was true."

"Were they good stories?" She bent down, hands on knees, and asked the little boy. "Did you like them?"

"They were the best stories ever," said the boy.

I wandered down Lovers' Lane, which begins behind Green Gables. By now more people had arrived at the park and I didn't have this trail to myself, as I had the Haunted Wood. Lovers' Lane weaves between trees and rocks and crosses a narrow stream several times. Again, it was easy to see how it had inspired Maud as a young writer. The lane features a few staircases to lookout platforms, and I climbed the ones that didn't have lines formed at the bottom as more people waited for their turn to explore every inch of the park.

When I left Lovers' Lane, I walked through the back yard to the gift shop before returning to the van. I'd planned to visit Avonlea Village, a recreation of Maud's invented setting for many of her books, but the Cavendish Beach Music Festival attendees occupied all parking spots within a reasonable (and unreasonable) distance. Avonlea Village would have to wait for my next trip to PEI.

I decided to continue on to Maud's birthplace and then the Anne of Green Gables Museum, both of which were included in the combination ticket I'd purchased before my trip.

Maud's birthplace site offered an interesting tour, a quick peek and walk-through, in New London, formerly known as Clifton, about seven miles west of Cavendish. This was a part of the Island I hadn't yet explored, situated among rolling farmlands and lupine-bordered roads. Maud's wedding gown is on display there, as well as some letters she wrote and other memorabilia.

The Anne of Green Gables Museum is located in Park Center, and it was the home of Maud's cousins, the Campbells, when she was growing up. This is where one can view the original Lake of Shining Waters, and wander through the rooms where Maud visited, sometimes for extended periods, during her childhood. Her handmade crazy quilt is on display here, among other personal items.

If I hadn't purchased the combination ticket, I may not have bothered to travel to these two remote sites. I'm glad I did, as it helped me envision Maud's life more fully and I appreciated her biography even more than I would have, had I not seen the places and walked the paths Maud herself had walked as a girl and a young woman. These places were more authentic than the manufactured Avonlea Village. I doubted I'd missed anything of substance.

After returning to the campground, I lugged my one load of laundry to the on-site laundromat. This required two trips into the camp store to purchase change, as I mis-read the sign and needed more loonies and no two-nies. I don't usually dry my clothes, preferring to hang them, so I carried wet clothes back to the van. Along the way, it started to sprinkle, so I installed my clothesline inside, anchoring one end in the bathroom and the other end on the edge of the cabinets above the table, and hung my clothes inside overnight. I trained the fan on them and ran the air conditioner for a while, and in the morning, all but a few shirts were dry enough to fold and stow.

The shirts remained on the clothesline while I drove around the next morning, giving me a laugh every time I glanced back. They bounced happily on the bungee cord, bright flags of joy waving around the van.

I felt like a gypsy! A nomad, roaming at whim.

Had I somehow morphed from a type A, uptight, overanxious, nauseatingly reliable person into someone who goes with the flow? I've always hated that term. It conjured images of garbage floating toward a storm drain.

Maybe it was my age—was this a midlife crisis? A hormonal imbalance? Yet another effect of global warming?

Whatever the cause, I felt happy. Truly happy. Not the giddy, barely contained excitement of a four-year-old shrieking and jumping for joy. Not that. This was a bone-deep contentment, a soul-hugging sense of peace and safety and confidence that stemmed from the knowledge that not only was I responsible for myself and no one else, I was also wholly responsible for my entire life. All of it, even the less desirable parts, were conceived in choices I'd made by and for myself. I felt triumphant.

*This must be what empowerment feels like*, I thought. *I like it.*

***

The next day, my last on PEI, began with a drive to Basin Head Beach. A light rain spattered the windshield, and when I arrived, the beach was nearly deserted. This beach is famous for its singing sands— the friction from bare feet trodding on the fine sand produces a pleasant hum, as if the sands are singing. I donned a light jacket with a hood and removed my shoes. My feet pattered along the beach, the now-familiar beautiful red sand pushing up between my toes. The sand warmed my feet as I walked. Stubborn wild rosebushes, vibrant fuchsia and green, clung to the rocky land near the beach. The roses were too far away to influence the scent of the saltwater— I inhaled deeply, enjoying the cool, fresh air. It was July 7 but it felt like early September.

I tried not to stare at the couple walking toward me on the beach. My eyes strained peripherally—who could help it? The woman wore a skirt, a light jacket and a hat, possibly just having rolled out of bed (it was 7 AM) for her morning stroll. Her husband, however, wore nothing but a tiny royal blue Speedo. He didn't need additional material in the front, but after we met and passed and I glanced around at them, I noted he could've used another few inches of coverage on the back side.

I toured my way along the coast from Basin Head Beach to Charlottetown. The shops and the beach in Souris warranted a lengthy walk and beach combing, even though it drizzled rain. I stopped at a garage sale and meandered through a couple of other small towns and arrived in Charlottetown hungry and tired.

Months earlier, I'd purchased tickets to tonight's live performance of Bittergirl, a musical comedy about getting dumped. After my long day in the rain, and the previous night, which I'd spent listening to my new campground neighbors reprimanding their children, I wasn't in the mood for a live performance. I was more in the mood to return to the campground and go to bed.

I checked the ticket. I'd paid $30 for it, so I decided to go to the first half of the performance and duck out during intermission if I didn't enjoy it.

*Bittergirl*, written by a Charlottetown playwright, relates the story of three women and their respective breakups with a sort of 'everyman' figure, played by one man. It features familiar tunes like "And Then He Kissed Me", "Ain't No Mountain High Enough", and

"Where Did Our Love Go". The three main characters are all phenomenal actresses, and their stories are shared through a series of witty skits and songs.

I stayed for the entire performance.

The Mack, a small downtown theatre, hosted the play. The audience sat at a smattering of round tables between the bar and the stage. There was a tiny drink station serving wine and beer set into a corner off of stage left with a prominent sign suspended above it reading The Whine Bar. Pure understated Canadian humor—my favorite kind. I didn't order wine, knowing I'd have to pilot the van back to the campground after the show. Two of the women at my table struck up a conversation and I learned one of them was moving two days later to Kitchener, Ontario, with her new boyfriend, also her high school sweetheart. She said they'd each married and had three kids, then divorced, and now they were together again, back where they'd started so long ago. I told them about my trip, and my van, and they said I was "one brave woman".

"You're the brave one," I said to the woman recently reunited with her high school beau. "You're throwing your lot in with a man again."

# Maine To New York To Michigan

I crossed Confederation Bridge the next morning at sunrise, not allowing myself to glance in the rearview mirror—if left to instinct, I might've turned around and stayed there. Right on PEI, where I could spend my days walking on sun-warmed beaches in search of jewelry-worthy beach glass. The girls I'd met at the Bittergirl performance said I looked like a local—I would easily blend into the Scottish immigrant island population.

The tug of responsibility being stronger than that of my fanciful dreams—so much for ditching my

Type A tendencies and embracing my inner gypsy—I crossed the border back into the USA and headed south on Highway US-1 until I happened upon a campground in Northport, Maine. They accepted cash only—$38.50 for full hook-ups at a large site with grand shade trees. It was hot and sticky when I stepped out of the van. I balanced the toaster oven on a pile of books so the short cord would reach the van's outside electrical outlet and baked a fresh quiche with the veggies I'd picked up at farmers' markets along the way. While it baked, I sipped wine and jotted notes about the day.

The border crossing, my fourth on this trip, had been easy, though I'd waited an hour in the lineup to approach the booth. By now I had my license plate number memorized, and I chatted with each customs officer about my vacation and how many people were lined up behind me. Sometimes the officer would step inside my rig and open random cupboards before letting me cross, but sometimes they would simply wave me through.

I continued south on US-1 the next morning. The scenery looked like a page from the LL Bean catalog: mountains, rocks, trees, ocean. Balsam and pine trees scented the air. I drove slowly, winding along the edge of the ocean, until I encountered the sign for Mount Battie at the Camden Hills State Park. Intrigued by the name, I pulled in and paid the $4 park entrance fee.

The summit of Mount Battie can be reached via

hiking trail or paved road. Since I hadn't yet finished my coffee and the sun hadn't quite crested the horizon, I drove up. And up. And up. At 800 feet above sea level, Mount Battie provides a grand view of Penobscot Bay and downtown Camden. There's a stone tower with an interior staircase that elevates visitors an additional twenty-six feet. The plaque on the front of the tower reads: *In grateful recognition of the services of the men and women of Camden in the World War, 1914-1918.*

I found another plaque nearby containing the first stanza of the poem "Renascence" by Edna St. Vincent Millay, followed by a brief paragraph: *At the age of eighteen, a frail girl with flaming red hair left her home in early morning to climb her favorite Camden Hills, where so deeply affected by her surroundings, she wrote "Renascence". The poem received immediate public acclaim and was the inspiring beginning of the career of American's finest lyric poet.*

I sat for a while—long enough to finish my coffee and contemplate this accidental discovery of Edna St. Vincent Millay's hometown. I'd read Nancy Milford's *Savage Beauty: The Life of Edna St. Vincent Millay* years before, but I'd forgotten that she'd lived in Camden.

I left the park and continued on US-1 until I came upon the most enchanting library I'd ever seen at the north end of town. The lush front lawn, cupola, and butter-cream columns compelled me to turn into the shaded lot and back into my parking space. It had clearly been waiting for me. The back yard of the library is an amphitheater, each row of seating made of grass with large rocks holding it in place. A yoga class was being conducted there as I walked by—the second yoga class I'd witnessed on this trip. Maybe the universe was trying to tell me something—I thought about my own yoga mat, stowed beneath the dinette bench in the van, unfurled thus far.

Following the woodland path around to the front of the library, I passed benches set up with a view of the marina below, bordered by rose bushes and other showy perennials. The library itself is an impressive structure, Colonial style with columns and bricks, welcoming all who seek comfort and knowledge. I browsed through their used books and bought one for my sister titled *The Last Bookaneer* by Mathew Pearl.

Between the library and the harbor, I encountered a bronze statue of Edna St. Vincent Millay. She stands facing the harbor, looking toward the sky, awaiting the next inspiration.

I walked the streets of Camden, browsing in the shops and chatting with other shoppers and store clerks. I bought a turquoise blue sweater with a large moose on it for myself and a few small gifts for others. Camden is the quintessential Downeast Maine town. It looked like a Martha Stewart magazine spread: every single home showcased horticultural perfection. Imagine the neighborhood botanistic pressure! I wondered: did the homeowners dig their own trowels into the dirt, or did they hire professional landscapers?

I continued down US-1 to Rockland, then Owls Head. I walked to the Owls Head Lighthouse and took photos of the ocean, then returned to Rockland for lunch at Archers on the Pier, an upscale waterfront restaurant. I ordered a Lobster Reuben (when in Maine...), but the waitress mistakenly entered it as a Haddock Reuben. I ate it without complaint, though. It was creamy and spicy and altogether fabulous, and so filling I only ate yogurt and popcorn for dinner later that night.

At some point, I'd realized my plans for pirouetting through Portland and blasting through Boston were way too ambitious and I'd crossed them off my itinerary. Maybe it was the luxuriously slow pace of my trip—I didn't want to thrust myself into city rush hours when I could continue to meander from town to village and explore at whim.

After lunch, I drove to Quechee, Vermont, near Woodstock. I stayed the night and explored the Quechee Gorge the next morning in the rain. Driving on, I found several covered bridges, one of which was too low for my ten-foot-tall van. I utilized the large turn-around area and headed back the way I came.

A local farmers' market offered a sale on perennials, and I bought a large fuchsia-colored hardy hibiscus plant to add to the garden along the side of my house. In my mind, this one addition would magically transform my meager plantings into a magazine-worthy garden like those in Camden, even as I feared it would die from neglect. I set in the shower so it wouldn't topple over.

By now, the check engine light glowing on the dashboard had become part of the charm of the Jan Van. I took my time on inclines so the engine wouldn't sputter, and my earlier panic now seemed like a waste of energy, as most panics do in hindsight. I still planned to pursue a remedy, but the sense of urgency had faded.

The drive from Quechee wound over hills, across rivers, past Victorian and Colonial houses in towns with park-like squares and lush landscaping. I settled for the night in Bainbridge, a small town in eastern New York near the southern end of the Finger Lakes Area.

This was another campground that advertised WiFi but the signal didn't reach my campsite. It barely reached the back yard of the office, but for $27 I had full hook-ups once again, so I didn't complain about the lack of signal. My campsite was right along the Susquehanna River, less than a hundred yards from the Interstate, but it was tucked below the road grade so highway sounds were muffled.

When I set up for the night, I pulled out the hibiscus and set it on the picnic table so I could admire it and water it. It was nearly ready to bloom, standing straight and tall about three feet above the top of the flower pot.

My new neighbor shuffled over to say hello. He looked about 90 years old and stood a solid four feet tall with his shoes on. I wondered how well he could see over the steering wheel of the F250 parked next to his fifth wheel trailer.

"Hi there. I'm Harold."

He extended a liver-spotted hand, and when I clasped it, he wrenched it up once, down once, then back to center. A slow motion handshake.

"Where you from?"

"Hi, Harold. Michigan."

"Yep. I used to live here. I worked at the leather factory for forty years." He folded his arms and rocked back on his heels. I got the feeling he'd delivered this speech before. "I been living in that trailer there since 2005. I live here in the summer and Daytona Beach in the winter. I haul that thing twice a year, and that's it."

I laughed. "You must like it here."

"Yep. And I have a ten-pound cat and a six-pound chihuahua. They're backwards. You know, they're sized wrong." He chuckled and hitched up his pants. He wore work pants, as if he'd just finished a shift at the factory. "Yep. Let me know if you need anything. I kind of manage the place after hours."

He was already heading back toward his trailer, so I called out to him. "Nice meeting you!"

I warmed up a piece of quiche and made a salad from the fresh veggies I'd purchased earlier and stationed myself at the picnic table facing the sunset. The hibiscus stood guard at my elbow.

"Is that your plant?" A man emerged from behind

the van and walked along the edge of the road.

"Yes." I glanced at him long enough to notice he had butterscotch-colored hair and wore a plaid button-down shirt with white-trimmed athletic shorts. I couldn't tell if he was slightly unhinged or just quirky. He looked about fifty-five years old. I quickly ate the last bite of my meal.

He stopped in the middle of the road, facing me. "That's kinda odd, isn't it? Traveling with a big old plant?"

"No." I felt uneasy. "Have a good evening." I said this in my best stern schoolmarm voice.

Why did these odd encounters keep happening? Was I crossing over from cautious to paranoid? *Better to overreact than under-react*, I thought. I grabbed my plate and potted flower and headed inside. I slid the door closed and pulled the blinds, then peeked out to make sure he walked away.

The sun set without me.

\*\*\*

The next day I drove about 500 miles to Dearborn, Michigan, to meet up with Jen and Todd and the kids. They had planned a weekend trip to tour Greenfield Village and the Henry Ford Museum, so I coordinated my schedule and met them at the hotel.

Mid-July isn't the best time to visit the Detroit area —it's hot and sticky and generally miserable. I briefly considered sleeping in the van in the hotel parking lot, but I needed to run the air conditioner, which would require running the generator, and I didn't want to make that much noise. I gathered everything I'd need for one overnight stay and settled into a hotel room for the night. It was worth the expense to stretch out in a real bed and relax in climate-controlled comfort.

The next morning, I rode to Greenfield Village with Jen and her family. An open air museum laid out like a small turn-of-the-century town, Greenfield Village showcases the innovations and inventions from the early twentieth century. Visitors can walk the streets or catch a ride on a Model T or a trolley, or even a horse-drawn carriage, and explore the various districts to learn about Henry Ford's life and the story of Ford Motor Company. There's a working nineteenth-century farm, a glassworks studio, and several restaurants. Thomas Edison's Menlo Park Complex and his Fort Myers Laboratory are here for visitors to explore.

According to Donald F. Wood in his book *RVs and Campers 1900-2000: An Illustrated History,* Henry Ford was one of the first to embark on a camping road trip. In 1915, he and Thomas Edison started taking annual camping road trips with a large group of friends, sometimes including Harvey Firestone, the naturalist John Burroughs, Luther Burbank, and Warren G. Harding. They would travel for a month or longer, and their first few trips included a truck outfitted with a refrigerator, a cook and small staff, and another truck for hauling tents, cots, folding chairs, lamps, and storage batteries. By their 1919 trip, Ford had fabricated two camping vehicles, one with a built-in kitchen and one to carry camping gear. Imagine the conversations they must have had around the evening campfires.

My favorite section of Greenfield Village was the Liberty Craftworks district, which features a glasswork studio, a machine shop, a weaving shop, and a pottery shop. Visitors can turn their own miniature metal candlesticks—a toothpick-sized candle might fit into one—and watch artisans blow glass and throw pots.

Greenfield Village has everything one might need, including several restaurants. We ate lunch at the Eagle Tavern, a mid-1800s-style place where a waiter in period costume served us. The menu, or Bill of Fare, offered "spiritous liquor" and "temperance beverages" as well as oyster fritters and dressed greens.

It was late afternoon by the time we returned to the hotel. Jen and Todd were taking the kids to visit Todd's cousin for the evening, and I was ready to head home. I'd been on the road for seventeen days.

I left just in time to catch a solid hour of rush hour traffic, and arrived home as the moon rose. I plugged in the van so the refrigerator would continue to run, walked inside the house, and fell into bed.

There's something uplifting about returning home from a lengthy trip. My house always seems more welcoming, more comfortable than I remember it. I think it misses me while I'm gone, and that's the best thing about returning.

Road Trip Rule # 33:

Bad experiences make
good stories.

MILE
1
5

# Michigan: Engine Troubles

After my epic PEI trip, I took a few short weekend trips to campgrounds closer to home. One morning, my arms full of groceries, I inadvertently pressed the door lock button three times and...the front doors locked, then unlocked. Locked, then unlocked. Locked. They stayed locked! This was such an exciting development I nearly dropped everything on the ground.

After discovering the secret of the key fob, I rarely

used it to lock the doors. Knowing I could lock the doors was nice, but it took about ten seconds to complete the entire lock sequence, and the locks were so loud they announced to everyone within two hundred feet that I was locking and unlocking the van. I continued to lock the doors from the inside and exit through the sliding door.

The van still struggled on inclines, both steep and not-so-steep. I found a Dodge dealer in Grand Rapids willing to look at it, so I planned a brief camping trip there. Google Maps showed a bike path near the dealership that led to a park where I could sit at a picnic table and watch dogs fetch frisbees. I hoped to claim a park bench and scribble a few words on my latest project.

Grand Rapids is about five hours from home, and I left the night before my appointment so I could arrive at the dealership before they opened. The weather canceled my planned bike ride with a cold blast of wind and needle-like rain, so I spent three hours in the cramped waiting room listening to CNN. Torch-wielding white nationalists had marched through the University of Virginia campus; someone had driven a car into the protesters in Charlottesville, killing one and wounding nineteen; Hurricane Harvey was on his way. All of this reminded me why I'd stopped watching the news. Clearly, more people needed to escape their chaotic lives and go camping. I pulled out my Kindle but it was difficult to concentrate with the television blaring in the corner and other customers milling about.

Finally, like a surgeon emerging from the operating room to notify the family, the mechanic came out and sat in the chair next to me. He'd been unable to determine what the problem was, or what was causing it.

My hope for a miracle cure leaked out and left me flattened, like a tire pierced by a metal shard.

"One of the hoses might have a pinhole in it, causing it to lose pressure," he said. This sounded like an easy problem to fix, but he explained the hoses were extremely difficult to access. They might need to remove the entire engine to locate the hose in question.

"Or…you might need a whole new transmission." His name tag read Dave. His empathetic gaze bored through the smudged lenses of his glasses. "I suggest you let the problem develop a bit longer. I expect it to gradually worsen—I don't think you'll end up stranded somewhere."

I dutifully transcribed as he talked, filling a page and a half in my Bullet Journal.

I explained how the problem had begun, moments after the Vermont shop had performed the recall repair, and he figured that was pure coincidence. He thought the previous owners might've had the same trouble and somehow managed to mask it.

He reset the check engine light but it lit up again five minutes after I left the dealership. I'd spent another $368 and still nothing was solved—or even diagnosed.

I pulled into the Woodland Mall parking lot to make lunch and decide where to go next. I opened the atlas to Michigan—it took up the entire table—while I ate my salad. Two people on bicycles raced toward me and circled the van. They appeared to be in their early twenties.

"This is it!" The woman yelled. Her long black hair tangled and whipped in the wind as she orbited the van.

I felt uneasy—did they know I was still inside? Were they planning to accost me when I exited? They didn't appear malicious. Were they friendly-seeming decoys for some unseen, sinister partner preparing to carjack the Jan Van?

"What?" Her companion called. His hair was black, too, as was the nascent beard marching across his face. He wore a yellow ball cap and untied high-top sneakers.

"It's a Mercedes!" The woman pumped her fist in the air. Her large owlish glasses and mulberry-colored winter jacket gave her a vintage flair. "That is so cool!"

"It's a motorhome!"

"A *Mercedes* motorhome! I want one!"

I laughed. Just a couple of kids out riding around. They zigzagged off across the parking lot, unaware of the troubles lurking behind the dazzling Mercedes emblem on the front grill.

It was still early when I left and wended my way up

Michigan's west coast through small artsy towns and past picturesque beaches. The weather didn't improve until I reached the Interlochen State Campground, when the clouds parted to reveal a spectacular sunset as I backed the van into my campsite. I built a fire with the small bundle of wood I'd purchased in the registration office and cooked my veggie burger in a burger press over the flames.

I read through the notes I'd taken while the mechanic had talked. They made little sense to me and I wondered how the problem would further develop. Would I lose power for longer periods of time, until I was forced to pull over? Would I be left stranded somewhere? Would I have to replace the transmission, or just a hose?

I gazed at my tidy little van. It remained stoic, unwilling to share any clues.

Road Trip Rule # 64:

Always pay attention.

# Wisconsin: Pumping Gas

As I waited for the transmission problem to develop, the Jan Van continued its feeble struggles on hills without worsening. I took another week off work and visited friends in Wisconsin, where I planned to meet my Aunt Karen, who had a Class B Chevrolet Road Trek. We planned to travel together for a few nights.

Driving north on Highway 51 in Wisconsin on a warm August morning, I approached Minocqua in search of fuel.

Aunt Karen was scouting campgrounds near Bayfield, a small town on Lake Superior, connected by ferry to the Apostle Islands, a place that had occupied my mom's travel wishlist for decades. So far, Karen had only encountered campgrounds with no vacancy and she'd learned that exploring the Apostle Islands requires planning ahead, which we hadn't realized.

My fuel tank was nearly empty. I spied a BP station with a diesel sign and pulled in. I didn't see the diesel pumps anywhere—the gas pumps were neatly lined up beneath a canopy and I crept by them, finally noticing a separate pump with a green handle on the other side of the station. While the fuel entered the tank, I thought about my upcoming trip with Aunt Karen while I glanced around.

*That's odd,* I thought. *Why did they label this pump 'gasoline'?* It took a moment for my brain to register the fact that I was pumping gas instead of diesel. I stopped the pump and Googled frantically, and quickly discovered gas might ruin my engine—or, it would be fine. The trusty internet, as usual, provided information at all levels of truth on the scale. I had pumped eleven gallons into the tank, which had been nearly empty. Some of the Google hits led to forums, and those forums mostly said if the gas was mixed with diesel, the engine would be fine. I pulled over to the diesel pump (which was clearly labeled, but only on the far end of the canopy where I couldn't have seen it when I first drove past). The tank took another fourteen gallons.

I sat in the driver's seat for a moment, afraid to start the van again, and called my brother-in-law while turning the key. The van started. I pulled out of the gas station as he answered.

"Hey, Todd. I have a dumb question for you."

"Okay."

"How bad is it if you put gasoline in a diesel tank?"

"Did you put gas in your van?"

"Maybe…"

"Don't drive it. Get it drained."

"Okay, I'll pull over right now."

"You're driving it? I can't believe it's even running. Maybe you've got enough diesel in there—but if not, it will wreck your engine."

"I'm pulling over." I braked and turned into a real estate office with a large parking lot. "Okay, I'm stopped. Engine is shut off."

"Let me know how you make out. Call a wrecker."

"Thank you."

I went inside the real estate office and met Mandy: coiffed, suited, and manicured. She'd been gazing into a pocket mirror and clapped it shut as I approached her desk. One errant eyebrow hair grew above her nose, but I trusted she'd already zeroed in on it.

I greeted her and introduced myself and told her I was traveling through town.

"I'm in a bit of a pickle," I said. "My van out there is diesel, and I put some gas in it. I need to have it towed and drained. Do you know who to call?"

Mandy knew who to call. She straightened her back and spoke as she tapped the phone with a perfect fingernail. "Earl will come and get you. He's the best tow truck driver—he's always busy. And there's a shop north of town that will probably be able to drain it for you. I'll give you their number."

She spoke to Earl's receptionist, who dispatched Earl immediately. He'd been standing by, waiting for a call.

"Here's the number for the shop—Earl said to call them before he gets here to make sure they can fit you in." She handed me a creamy notecard on which she'd written, in perfect script, the name and number of the mechanic.

"Thank you so much," I said. "You've really helped me out. And I love your nails."

She glanced at her coral-tipped fingers—one nail was metallic copper—and smiled. "Thank you. I do them myself. It's one good thing about working here." She glanced around. "There's a lot of down time."

I thanked her again and walked outside to wait for Earl. I texted Todd while I waited to let him know I had a tow truck on the way, and called the shop whose number Mandy had provided. They could fit me in. Everything was falling into place, which seemed lucky if I didn't consider why I needed all of these things to fall into place. Distracted gas pumping: Had I discovered the next driving hazard?

Earl pulled into the parking lot about fifteen

minutes later and lifted the rear end of my vehicle with his tow truck while I took pictures of the Jan Van in its compromising position.

"You'd best hop into the cab, there." Earl pointed to the tow truck. "I'd shake yer hand, but I'm greasy." He held up two blackened hands for proof. "Hazard of the job."

"No problem. I'm just glad you had time for a rescue."

He grinned at me, his teeth a yellow swath across his black-stubbled face. "I always make time for the ladies."

Earl looked old enough to be my father, so I took his comment as the inoffensive joke I assumed he'd intended. Not only was I raised under a sexist umbrella that normalized derogatory remarks, I was the first female to hold a traditionally male position at my company. When I arrived at a job site, one of two things would happen: I'd be treated with derision until the client realized I actually knew what I was doing, or I'd be greeted with a surprised look and become the subject of several effusive remarks about how grand it was that I was doing this job. At some point, I'd stopped concerning myself with other people's attitudes and turned a deaf ear to their sexist ramblings.

"Brad's Auto say they can drain your tank?"

"Yes. I talked to Brad himself and he said he can do it in an hour or so."

"I'll have you there in ten minutes."

"Thanks again. I can't believe I did that—the pump is over on the north side of the gas station, and I assumed it was diesel. I don't think I even looked at the label. It was E85!"

"Don't feel too bad." Earl patted the seat between us. I was thankful he didn't reach across and touch my leg. "Even *men* put gas in their diesel tanks sometimes."

I stifled a laugh. "Well, that makes me feel better," I said, again deciding not to take offense. Wasting my energy on Earl and his sexist philosophy would change nothing.

Earl turned onto a side road and I spied the sign for Brad's Auto Shop. The road was about one and a half lanes wide with a sharp slope toward a stagnant pond. Brad's parking lot, at pond level, could be accessed from either end. Earl drove to the far end, with the steeper approach. The driveway was paved but the gravel along the edge had been washed out and now a deep crevice bordered the blacktop—a tire-wide luge-run headed straight down the slope. If a tire dropped off the driveway, the steep incline would dispatch the van directly into the bog at the edge of the parking lot.

We pulled up on the street and Earl cranked the wheel to back the van downhill into the parking lot. He cut the corner so close one of the van's tires skated off the edge of the driveway. He threw his truck into drive and jerked it forward onto solid ground.

Visions of a slow motion rollover crowded my head. The van would've rolled down the embankment and into the pond. It would've become fish habitat, or swamp thing habitat, or whatever lived in that cesspool. I took a long slow breath and hopped out of the tow truck to join Earl as he disconnected the van and steered it downhill and into place.

"Driveway's too steep," said Earl. He wiped his blackened hands on the blackened rag he kept stuffed in his back pocket. "Sorry if I alarmed you. It's a tricky landing." He shook his head. "Makes ladies nervous."

As if he'd *planned* to nearly dump my van off the incline and into the pond? How dumb did he think I was? I could only endure so much sexism on one day.

"You can't expect too much of us ladies," I said. "Between our gas pumping skills and parking abilities, we're lucky you men allow us to drive on public roads."

Even ladies get the last word, sometimes.

"Right?" Earl nodded, his grin revealing two missing back teeth, a nice match for his vacant brain. "You know what? I'm a-gonna give you a deal. It's just $180 for the tow today."

"Thank you, Earl. And thanks for the rescue. I appreciate it."

I paid Earl by calling his secretary Wendy and giving her my credit card number while he visited with Brad, further delaying my repair.

"Thanks, doll." Wendy's nasal voice was

punctuated with gum chewing and popping sounds and she spoke as if every sentence was a question. "We tried to let Earl have an iPad so he could take credit cards? But he broke like three of those things? So now we just hope he can operate the phone. Know what I mean?"

"As long as we let them think they're running the world, everything will work out."

Wendy screeched. "Exactly! Now you have a good weekend, doll. Drive safe out there."

Brad checked my fuel tank and determined he'd have to put the van on the hoist to drain it. Some tanks apparently have a handy drain built-in, but mine wasn't one of them.

"This won't take long," he said. "And don't feel bad. We've got a guy in town who does this every year."

"Really?"

"Oh, yeah. When I heard what had happened, I was expecting to hear Rod's voice." Brad shook his head. "We'll have you out of here in about thirty minutes."

Meanwhile, Aunt Karen had checked several campgrounds and found no vacancies. I called a couple of places while my tank was being drained, and found two available sites at a campground near Boulder Junction, Wisconsin.

"What's it called?" Aunt Karen had pulled over to program her GPS.

"Camp Holiday," I said. "The photos look better

than the name implies."

"It's a bit on the nose." She laughed. "But maybe tourists like obvious cues better than vague ones."

We laughed and I told her about my gas/diesel debacle, ending with the statement Earl had made about "even men" putting gas into diesel tanks.

"Wait, so you're as dumb as a man now?"

"It would seem so."

"I'm sure you'll revert to your smart female self after a good night's sleep at Camp Holiday."

Aunt Karen is my mom's sister and lifelong best friend. Despite living hundreds of miles apart most of their adult lives, Karen and Mom visited back and forth a few times per year and talked on the phone weekly. Karen has three sons, two of whom live near her in Alaska, and one who resides in the southwestern corner of Michigan. She drives her Road Trek from Alaska to Michigan each summer to visit the few of us family members who haven't migrated to Alaska.

Camp Holiday is a large family-owned campground a few miles outside of Boulder Junction. Situated on Rudolph Lake, it has over 350 sites, a beach, a fish cleaning station, and three bath houses. The office building has a game room and a small camp store, and the owners are chatty and jolly. There are a few sites with established seasonal campers, but most of the sites are reserved for a few nights at a time.

Karen walked in the office door as I was finishing

my reservation. We both chose sites with full hook-ups on the same street. There weren't two adjoining sites available, but we weren't too far apart.

We left the office and drove to our respective sites to set up. I plugged in, hung my curtains, and carried a tray of provisions to Karen's camper. She was sitting outside with her dog Makki, enjoying the late summer breeze and watching other campers.

We combined our various snack foods into a colorful array on a large tray and ate while we talked. Makki monitored the campground from her position near the bumper, where Karen had attached her leash. Makki is half golden retriever and half husky—very friendly, with enough exuberance for at least three dogs.

"Before I bought this van, I had convinced myself I wouldn't like camping at these large parks," she said. "But now that I've stayed at a few of them, I discovered I quite enjoy it." She poured us each a glass of wine.

"It's fun to people-watch at these places," I said. "And I like taking a walking tour to see how everyone else sets up. It's really the only place you can stare without being rude. Sometimes I learn something I can use in my own set-up." I filled a small plate with cheese, crackers, olives, hummus, carrots, and grapes.

"The permanent set-ups are elaborate," said Karen.

"I noticed a few of those on my way here—wood decks, flowers and vegetables growing in pots, and one had a carport for the pick-up truck."

"That one has a sidewalk and patio." Karen pointed to a site across the way. The owners had laid patio pavers in an elaborate design, and they had a small garden between the road and the trailer.

"Wow. I wonder how long they've been here."

"One of my favorite things about having this little house on wheels is the ability to move at whim, and change my scenery whenever I feel like it," she said.

"Me too. My regular house is already rooted. Why would I want two houses with fixed addresses? And the ever-changing scenery is the best part of traveling in my mini house."

\*\*\*

As much as I loved the Jan Van, Aunt Karen's Road Trek has some enviable features: a hinged entry door instead of a sliding door; two roomy twin beds in the back that easily convert into Queen-sized comfort; and another set of doors at the rear, handy when hauling large items. The Road Trek's fatal flaw is the wet bathroom. Aunt Karen has never showered in her van.

The next morning, we cruised through Boulder Junction when the day's festivities were scheduled to begin, but we were unable to find parking spots within walking distance of the fair. We continued toward Michigan, heading north on Highway 45 to Watersmeet, where we stopped at Nordine's Foodland for brunch.

"Where shall we go next?" I asked Aunt Karen.

We pulled out our phones to check the map.

"Doesn't matter to me," she said. "I'm thoroughly enjoying this caravanning thing. It's so relaxing—I just follow your tall white van. I don't have to think about anything." She grinned. "I gave Gara the day off."

"Gara?"

"My GPS." She rolled her eyes. "She was overworked anyway. Always behind. Constantly recalculating."

We headed east on US-2 to Norway, where we poked through a couple of shops and let the dog out for a few minutes. I found a campground on the north side of Iron Mountain with vacancy, and we headed back there on US-2.

It was a perfect evening at the Summer Breeze Campground—no wind, and warm enough to wear short sleeves. We stationed ourselves near the campfire and sipped wine while we planned for the next day.

"I think we should go up to L'Anse. I haven't stopped there in ages," said Aunt Karen.

"Except for lunch one day when I was eight years old, I've never stopped in L'Anse," I said. "Whenever we went to the cabin, we stopped in Marquette. Once in a while we stopped in Munising, but never in L'Anse."

"They have a cute main street along the water." She studied the Michigan page in the atlas. "We could head up to Skanee. I've never been to Skanee, and I always wondered about it when I saw the sign on M-28 as I sailed through L'Anse."

I grinned. "Skanee. What in the world is in Skanee?"

The next day, we did just that—we found a nice park in L'Anse and ate leftover quiche for lunch, then we left the dog in Aunt Karen's van and walked down the main street. There aren't many stores there, but we found an art supply store with low prices and a chatty clerk.

"This is a dangerous place for me to hang out," said Aunt Karen. She's a painter and sketch artist, and her work has been featured in many art galleries in Michigan and Alaska. Most of her shows feature her scenery pieces: Alaskan mountains and fjords, Michigan birch trees, the view from a Canadian mountaintop. She always carries a sketch book with her and draws whatever catches her fancy—people, trees, scenery. For a while she drew an entire cadre of fairies, and she's currently enamored with wild and crazy flowers, a species she created.

"I'm into acrylic paint these days." She held up a package of paints to show me the sale price.

"No more watercolor?"

She shrugged. "I got tired of watercolor. I've moved on."

"Acrylic might be better for your commercial line, when you're ready." I thought she should print notecards, book bags, and coasters with some of her artwork, but she refused to sell anything except originals. No prints of any kind.

"That's still against my policy," she said.

We left the art store with small bags of loot, returned to our vans, and drove to the grocery store.

"Those two look like locals." Aunt Karen gestured toward a man and woman setting groceries into the back of an old green Ford pickup. She walked over and asked them if they knew of a good campground near Skanee.

"There's Witz Marina," said the woman. "They have campsites right next to the boat slips."

I tapped the location into my campground app, but it wasn't listed.

"It's about twenty minutes up the road," said the man. "Watch for the signs. You'll turn on Witz Road, and then you can't miss it."

"Worth a try," said Karen. "Thank you!"

We grabbed a few groceries and drove up Skanee Road to Witz Road, and easily found Witz Marina. It's a family-owned marina and campground, and the sites really are perched on the edge of the docks. There were a handful of vacancies—we chose sites with water and electricity hook-ups and a Lake Superior view for $25. In our haste to discover this local treasure, we'd forgotten to purchase wine (an unprecedented event). Neither of us realized we lacked libations until after we had set up our vans for the night, so we walked to the camp store to see how far we'd have to backtrack to buy some campfire-sipping wine. The campground owner, Scott, ferried us to the nearest store and back in his car.

"You can't beat Yooper hospitality," said Aunt Karen, referring to those of us from the UP by our collective nickname.

Scott smiled and shrugged. "I had to run to the store anyway."

We finally returned to our campsites, prepared a tray of fresh fruits, veggies, cheese, crackers, and chocolate, poured the wine, and built a campfire. A light rain started falling—enough to make the fire spit, but not enough to kill the flames. We sat under my awning and sipped wine while the fire flashed and sizzled, until the rain gave up and we moved closer to the fire. This was our last night together.

The next morning, Aunt Karen joined me for coffee. I offered her a hot refill, but the van door wouldn't budge when I tried to open it.

"Are you locked out?" Asked Aunt Karen.

I glanced at her over my shoulder. "I can't be—the sliding door can only be locked from the inside. It's a manual lock."

"You must've bumped it on your way out."

I tugged a couple more times on the door. I tried sliding it farther shut in case the latch hadn't quite released; I tried sliding it open slowly, then quickly. Nothing moved.

"I must have. I have no idea how."

"So, where's your spare key?"

I grinned at her. "It's in the van, of course. Safe

and sound."

"What's the plan? I know you have one." She sipped her coffee.

"I think I can open the window over the bed far enough to fit through it."

"This is great—thank you so much for providing this morning's entertainment. I wasn't expecting such an elaborate performance!" She chuckled.

"No problem! And no charge, either." I walked around to the other side of the van and tried to slide the window open. It wouldn't budge. I walked back to the passenger side, where Karen sat at the picnic table, and tried the window above the dinette table. It slid smoothly open.

"Not the most secure vehicle in the fleet," said Aunt Karen.

"It's good to be able to break into your own stuff," I said. I used the back tire as a step and went in head first, careful not to put too much weight on the wobbly table.

I emerged a moment later with a hot carafe of coffee and we each had one more cup before departing the campground.

Aunt Karen headed west to visit a friend in Ontonagon and I headed east toward home.

# Wayside Ahead:
# Free Overnight Parking, Dry
# Camping, and Boondocking

When I spend the night in a store parking lot, I try to arrive at dusk or after dark. I park facing away from others and install the front curtains before turning on the interior lights so no one will know I'm traveling solo. Sometimes I turn the TV on for a few minutes to mimic conversation, but usually I just read a book for a while before turning in. I don't exit the van until morning, when I will enter the store to buy a few things as a thank you for the hospitality.

There are some unspoken rules regarding parking overnight at a store such as Walmart or Cabela's. It's understood that you're allowed to park—not camp. That means no chairs set up in the parking lot, no grilling outside, no loud noises. Most campers don't run generators after dark in a store parking lot unless it's hot and humid and they need to run their air conditioners. Few stores are willing to extend the courtesy of a free overnight parking spot to RVers who aren't the most gracious of guests.

I haven't yet had any problems while parked overnight at the stores that allow RVers to stay, and I'll continue to seek out those stores when I just need a parking space without hookups. There are several phone apps that indicate which stores allow overnight parking.

In addition to store parking lots, there are groups that offer a free parking spot, usually without hook-ups, for an annual fee. One group, Harvest Hosts, offers free camping spots at wineries, farms, golf courses, and other small businesses. When you pay their annual fee, which is around $50, you can access their database of hosts. The general procedure is to call in the afternoon to see if they have vacancy that night, and make arrangements on the spot. If they have a store on site, a purchase is expected in return for their hospitality. A few of these hosts offer electric hook-ups, but most of them just provide a flat place to park. I belonged to Harvest Hosts for a year, but it didn't work well for me because of the locations of the hosts and the last-minute nature of their reservations. I did stay at some interesting places that year, though, including a winery in Maine and a maple syrup farm in Vermont.

Staying with a Harvest Host is closer to dry camping than just free parking—many of them don't mind if you set up chairs outside and some of them provide campfire rings. Each one is different—you can read their rules and preferences on the Harvest Hosts app or website, or talk to the hosts when you arrive. At the winery in Maine, I arrived near the end of their wine tasting event. I sipped a few different wines, bought two, and was directed to park next to the horse corral. They encouraged me to walk up the path past the greenhouse to watch the sunset and visit the sheep. I had no hook-ups and no campfire ring, and I was parked in a meadow of knee-high grass and wildflowers, but it was a lovely place to spend the night. Until I returned from my visit to the sheep corral, when the horses commenced neighing and snorting. There were only three horses, but at least two of them were chatterboxes—possibly gossiping about the sheep—and they continued to neigh and snort throughout the night.

When you camp in the wilderness without hook-ups, such as on Federal land or on someone's back forty, that's considered boondocking. You might have an entire campsite set up: outdoor rug, campfire ring, chairs, screen tent, picnic table. There are more opportunities for this in the western US than in the areas I've traveled.

Road Trip Rule # 73:

Learn something every day.

## Michigan: Lone Wolf

On the way home from my visit with Aunt Karen, I backed into my chosen site at the Munising Tourist Campground, on a sandy Lake Superior beach just west of Munising, Michigan. I'd need to hurry if I wanted to walk the beach before sunset.

"Are you a lone wolf, like me?"

I hadn't noticed the willowy woman approach. She had white frizzy hair pulled into a messy bun and one hand gripped a short leash tethering a labradoodle.

He sat down while we talked.

"Yes, I'm traveling solo," I said. I walked over and offered my hand. "I'm Jan."

She shook my hand and said, "Amelia. From Texas." She nodded at the van. "I used to own a Mercedes Sprinter."

"What do you have now?"

"A Ford Transit—I'm in site twelve, if you want to come over for a tour and a beverage after you're set up."

"I might take you up on that. Why didn't you get another Mercedes?"

She waved her hand, jangling her bracelets. "Nothing but trouble. Nobody would work on it, and if they did, they charged the earth and didn't fix it properly."

"I'm running into the same thing."

"Buy something else. As soon as you can. Best thing I ever did." She gestured toward the dog, who stood up. "Come on, Rufus." She looked back at me. "We won't hold you up. Pop over when you're settled in."

I walked by her site later, but she'd already tucked in for the night. She was gone before I pulled out the next morning. Perhaps our paths had crossed for the sole purpose of sharing her story of similar experiences with a used Mercedes van.

MILE
1
8

# Michigan: A Day With Dad

My first camping season with the Jan Van had ended and I hadn't yet shown it to Dad. Before stowing it for the cold months, I drove to his place near Petoskey, in the tip of Michigan's Lower Peninsula mitten. As I guided the van into the far end of the lot at the veterans' retirement home a lone maple leaf drifted down onto my windshield as if to remind me winter was on its way.

Dad was sitting on the couch in the lobby

watching a movie on the big screen television with four other residents. One I recognized as Enid, pulling on her left earlobe and repeating every actor's line a half-beat behind. Margaret stood next to Dad's chair as if waiting for an invitation to sit. The other two, Harold and Agnes, had nodded off and slumped toward each other on the couch. Dad wore his Australian outback hat, a leftover relic from his nickel-prospecting days Down Under, and the vest his mother had knitted for him when he was twenty-two —fifty-five years before. It still fit perfectly. He looked ready to leave, for the afternoon or forever.

"Hey, Dad," I perched on the edge of a chair. I'd recently begun calling him Dad again, about five years after we'd reconnected. It was starting to feel more natural, although he had changed so much it sometimes felt like he was someone else's father.

"Hello." He smiled and slapped his hands down on his knees. "Are we going somewhere today?"

"I thought I'd take you for a ride through the Tunnel of Trees," I said. "And we'll do lunch at Legs Inn."

"Tunnel of trees," said Enid.

"Ooh, that's a nice ride, John," said Margaret. She patted his shoulder.

Dad stood up and started walking toward the door, waving goodbye over his shoulder.

I hastily signed Dad out so the cafeteria staff wouldn't prepare his lunch, and found him outside waiting for me.

"I brought my van today. I thought you'd like to see it, and take a ride in it."

"Very good," said Dad. He started across the parking lot at his usual fast pace, thumping his cane down with every other step. He'd carried a cane since his hip replacement, but it was more of a precaution than a necessity. It was tethered to his belt loop with a small nylon rope so it wouldn't clatter on the floor if he dropped it.

I opened the door and stepped into the camper, and Dad easily clambered in behind me.

"It's not new," I said. "But it has a Mercedes Diesel, and everything I need to stay wherever I want." I didn't reveal the van's mechanical infirmities, although at one time he probably would've been able to repair it. Or at least, he would've known if it was the entire transmission or just a pinhole in a hose that required attention.

"This is fantastic," he said in approval, a satisfied smile on his face.

His approval wasn't the coveted, hard-earned reward it had once been, but I enjoyed it nonetheless.

I showed him the cooktop, the tiny fridge, and the microwave. We sat for a moment in the dinette and looked out the window at the grasses waving in the breeze.

"Where are we going?" He asked.

He'd forgotten already. I never knew if I should repeat short phrases when he forgot things, or give him more information to fill in some of the blanks.

More bits for his mind to grab and examine. This time I opted for more information.

"The Tunnel of Trees." I gestured with one hand. "We'll leave Petoskey and go through Harbor Springs, then take M-37, also known as the Tunnel of Trees, up the coast of Lake Michigan. It's a beautiful drive, especially this time of year."

"Fantastic," he said again.

We took our seats and I pulled out of the parking lot.

"Remember when we took the Rolls K'Nardly to New Mexico?" I asked.

Dad grinned. "We burned through a dozen fan belts on that trip."

I laughed. "I remember one night we slept in the police station parking lot in some town in Kansas."

"It was the only safe-looking place I could find," he said, with a mock frown and a quick eye-roll.

It was difficult to tell where in time Dad's personal reality existed. He seemed to understand that I was in my forties, but he also spoke about his boyhood pet, Prince, as if the dog was still alive. He sometimes thought my sister was four years old, but never seemed to forget that I was an adult. He believed he was still in the service and awaiting orders, even though his brief time in the Navy had occurred before college. Dad had experienced a lack of oxygen to the brain at some point in the recent past that left him with diminished mental capacity—a form of non-Alzheimer's dementia without a name of its own.

At the same time, he'd developed a pleasant outlook and replaced his standard scowl with a ready smile, and it had taken my sister and me some time to adapt.

He looked comfortable riding shotgun and I was reminded of the first time I'd driven a car, when he had pulled off the highway about thirty miles from home, and told me to move over and take the wheel. We were in my grandma's old Plymouth Duster, which she'd given to Mom when she bought herself a new car. It was fire engine red and had black and white houndstooth cloth seats. I was twelve years old. I cautiously accelerated and turned the wheel while whipping my head around to watch for cars. We sailed past the farms with a slight weave, but I stayed within our lane, even on the curves.

We'd been tight back then, my dad and me, before the unsuitable boyfriend, before the curfew cutting and the midnight window exits. Before I moved out and he legally disowned me. Before the ensuing nineteen years of silence and anger and resentment and regret, none of which was ever mentioned aloud after our fragile reconciliation.

Now, I gripped the van's steering wheel and thought about how far we'd come since that first driving lesson, and how much we'd never know about each other's lives. How many memories we'd never share.

"I'm glad you showed me this," said Dad. He was smiling and looking right at me, his ice blue eyes clear and full of joy.

"The van? Yeah, I love it. It's perfect for one person."

"The van and the Tunnel of Trees. I really appreciate you visiting me, and taking me out."

There was a time, before the dementia, when Dad never would have uttered a phrase of gratitude. He'd had high standards for himself and everyone around him, and he'd barely acknowledged perfect grades and other academic achievements. His discipline system consisted of punishing our failures, while Mom's discipline system was predicated on lavish praise for our successes, no matter how small.

"No problem, Dad. I needed an excuse to drive on this road. Doesn't it feel like we're flying past these trees?" The trees were indeed flashing past the van, and some of the branches grazed the roof as we glided by. The road is narrow with virtually no shoulders, and the trees are just a few inches from the blacktop in places. We were going 35 mph.

He nodded. "I wouldn't want to drive a much bigger rig through here."

Just then, we met a Class A motorhome coming toward us. I inched the van over to hug the edge of the blacktop, mindful of the tree trunks threatening to destroy the side mirror. Dad remained at ease, enjoying his close-up view of the hardwoods as we threaded our way toward Good Hart and Cross Village. The Class A passed us by in a whoosh, leaves dancing in its wake.

Dad and I arrived at Legs Inn, which is worth the

drive from just about anywhere in the United States. It's in Cross Village, on Michigan's west coast, and it boasts a Polish menu with lots of Great Lakes fish entrees and a couple of vegetarian choices. On the outside, it's a stone cottage squatting on the side of the road. On the inside, the walls are lined with animal heads and the ceiling is lined with stove legs. The breeze off the lake was too chilly for us to sit on the garden patio. We went inside and chose a table.

Dad, with my assistance, ordered the Waugoshance Salad, which featured smoked whitefish. I had the Greys Reef Salad.

"This place hasn't changed a bit," said Dad. He glanced around the room in appreciation, studying the moose and deer heads. He'd never been there before, but I didn't tell him that.

We finished our meals, passing the time with small talk, which is the highest level of conversation he could manage, and the only kind of conversation our fractured history could endure. We took the same route back to his place, the sun playing peekaboo through the trees and sparkling on the Lake Michigan waves.

It was an ordinary day by all accounts, but it was an extraordinary and poignant day to me.

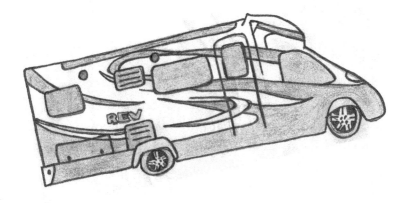

# CLOSE
# ENCOUNTERS

Road Trip Rule # 25:

These are the good old days.

MILE
1
9

## Michigan: Losing Dad

I lost my dad for the second and final time on a stark Thursday afternoon in February. Five months after our drive through the Tunnel of Trees. Winter was relentless that year and back-to-back blizzards had prevented Jen and me from visiting Dad for a few weeks. By that time, I had decided to purchase a brand new rig and I was mired in the search.

On Tuesday morning, he failed to show up for breakfast in the dining area of his assisted living complex. An attendant found him sitting on the floor of his apartment, disoriented and struggling to breathe. The ambulance rushed him to the hospital, mere blocks away, and by the time the manager from the assisted living place called to alert me, he was breathing through an oxygen mask.

My sister and I left work and headed for the hospital only to discover the Mackinac Bridge, which links the upper and lower peninsulas of Michigan, was closed due to high winds. I left a message for the doctor, who called me back several hours later.

"He's very fit and flexible for his age," said the doctor. "But his lungs are in a sorry state. If he survives the pneumonia, he'll likely be on oxygen for the rest of his life."

I wrote as he spoke, my words filling an entire page in my Bullet Journal. Mycoplasma pneumonia had invaded Dad's lungs, which were further compromised by underlying emphysema. He'd tested negative for emphysema a scant year earlier, despite his sixty-year smoking habit.

"That brings me to the difficult part," the doctor continued. "We have to discuss whether or not you want a DNR order for your dad."

I'd watched enough Grey's Anatomy to know what DNR meant: Do Not Resuscitate.

"He's only 77," I said. "And he's otherwise healthy. Yes, please resuscitate if necessary."

Silence. For nearly a minute.

"The thing most people don't know about the

resuscitation procedure is the after-effect on the patient."

Another painfully long pause. I counted ten thudding heartbeats before he spoke again.

"We've given your dad three liters of oxygen so far. His blood oxygen level is now hovering between 92 and 98 percent, which is good. The trouble is, we've had to increase his oxygen as the hours tick by. With his smoking history and the severity of the pneumonia, there's a chance he'll go into respiratory failure."

The doctor spoke clearly and evenly, with kindness and respect. I scrawled down everything he said so I could absorb it later.

"At that point, we would intubate him, then put him on a ventilator."

"Okay." That sounded reasonable.

"In cases like this, even though he's healthy otherwise, the chances of recovering and coming off the ventilator are extremely low. He can only be intubated for fourteen days, and after that we'd have to go through the trachea to keep him on the ventilator."

"Oh, my."

"Yes." The doctor sighed. "Unfortunately, the news gets worse. He's tired, and we're afraid his respiratory muscles will simply give out. There's so much damage to his respiratory system, he probably wouldn't survive CPR if he experienced heart failure."

Dad had granted medical power of attorney to me

so I could make decisions like this, should he be incapacitated. How could I possibly choose not to resuscitate my father? How did others deal with this kind of conundrum? I felt ill-equipped, inept. Unprepared.

"It seems like there's no good choice," I said to the doctor. "What would you do if it was your father?"

The doctor was ready for this question. "I propose aggressive medical care. We'll give him medication to slow his respiration so he won't have to work so hard to breathe. We'll give him antibiotics and steroids, and breathing treatments as needed. And of course, we'll keep him on oxygen. I don't want to sound too gloomy—there is a chance he'll recover from this. But if we had to resuscitate, he would not be the same person he is now. He would possibly suffer some brain damage and perhaps some personality changes. If he was my father," he paused, "I would sign a DNR."

I gave the doctor my verbal consent for a DNR. It hollowed me out. Intellectually, I knew I'd made the correct choice. Emotionally, it felt like I was sentencing my dad to death—like I was permanently rejecting him. This felt far worse than his rejection of me, when he'd legally disowned me thirty-one years prior.

"One more thing," I said to the doctor. "For the last twenty years of his career, Dad was an RN in the coronary care unit at a VA hospital. You can talk to him about his situation. Let him read his own chart, if you can."

"Oh, that's good to know! He seemed familiar with the oxygen machine. He was pushing the buttons last night as if he was reprogramming it."

I laughed. "He's always liked to take things apart and put them back together. They usually work better after he does it, too. He once built a ham radio—he soldered every little component. Before he was an RN, he was a geophysicist."

The doctor reassured me I'd made the right decision and we ended the call.

The next morning, Jen and I arrived at the hospital when visiting hours began. We donned face masks and coated our hands with sanitizer as instructed by the nurse before entering Dad's room. I steeled myself in case he didn't recognized our mask-obscured faces, but he immediately gestured for us to come in and sit down. He was breathing through an oxygen mask and pressing buttons on the remote control with a distracted and compulsive urgency.

He'd apparently stopped shaving during the three weeks of serial snow storms that had just blazed through the area. I wondered if this was an indication his dementia had advanced—had he forgotten that shaving was part of his daily routine? Did he notice the changes in the mirror every day? It seemed unlikely the beard had been a conscious choice.

His full white beard lent him a professorial look, but I worried the facial hair would reduce the oxygen mask's efficacy and create a habitat for bacteria.

The nurse replaced the mask with a canula so he could more easily speak to us.

"He usually shaves," I told the nurse. "If the facial hair is problematic, he won't mind if you shave it off."

Dad nodded and smiled in agreement, but the nurse was unconcerned.

"It's not a problem yet," she said.

Jen and I spent the day sitting with Dad—or, rather, encouraging Dad to sit. Every few minutes he'd hop out of bed and play musical chairs, perching on each one for a few seconds and tangling his oxygen hose in the process. When his lunch arrived, every bite he conveyed to his mouth fell out onto his hospital gown. The same thing happened when he tried to drink water—it dribbled down his chin in a most undignified manner.

After a while, the canula wasn't providing enough oxygen and the nurse reinstalled the oxygen mask. Throughout these setbacks and challenges, Dad remained jovial. We'd brought him a palm-sized puzzle with parts that twisted in different directions, a new focus for his fidgety hands. The television on the wall opposite his bed was tuned to the winter Olympics and every now and then he'd gesture at the screen with an expression of admiration or disappointment.

We sat on metal folding chairs—evidently the hospital suffered a furniture shortage—alongside his bed, careful not to encroach on his personal space. Dad had always been standoffish, aloof. We called him the iceman. He wasn't just socially chilly; his core body temperature was 97.6 Fahrenheit, a full degree colder than average.

After Dad pulled his oxygen mask off a couple of times, one of the nurses stationed herself on the other side of his bed and cozied right up to him. She leaned toward his face until he had no choice but to look at her, and I felt Jen's anxiety synchronize with my own and ratchet upward.

"My name is Lisa," she said to Dad. She nodded toward us as well.

"I'm Jan," I said. I held one hand toward my sister. "And this is Jen."

"You have very nice daughters, John." Lisa said to Dad. She trumpeted loud, slow syllables three inches from his face, the stethoscope looped around her neck threatening to graze his chest. "Your daughters came here to visit you today."

Even as he smiled and nodded at Lisa, we braced ourselves for a blowout. Dad required an arm's length of personal space, and there was no way for him to retreat or reposition himself. No available exit. We silently rehearsed the apologies and explanations we would offer Lisa when he spewed the litany of insults and reprimands we knew were coming.

But it didn't happen. He didn't blow up. He continued to smile, and even calmed a bit and stopped fidgeting with the toy we'd given him. That's when we noticed Lisa was *holding his hand.*

We'd never seen such a thing. We had seen

attempts over the years, when people—strangers—approached Dad and stood too close or shook his hand too long or (gasp) trapped him in a hug. However, we had never dreamed we'd witness him tolerate such overtures. And he wasn't just tolerating Lisa's touch. He was gripping her hand like it was a lifeline.

I realized I'd stopped breathing at some point, and felt mildly dizzy. I gulped some air through the mask. "I need coffee." I turned to Jen. "Do you want to run to the cafeteria with me?"

Her big blue eyes were bigger and bluer than they'd ever been as she looked at me over her mask. "Yes."

We left the room and found the doctor after silently agreeing neither of us really needed coffee.

His face looked grim. "Your dad is in a serious battle. Sixty years of smoking." He shook his head. "His chickens are coming home to roost."

"His blackened, burned out, breathless chickens," I said.

The doctor was happy with the course we'd chosen and he wanted to continue.

"My main concern is his rest," said the doctor. "He hasn't slept a wink since he arrived here yesterday."

We stopped back into Dad's room for a moment before leaving for the evening. He and Lisa were huddled together on the far side of his bed.

We interrupted her murmurs to wish Dad a good night.

"I'll see you girls tomorrow," he said, waving us out of the room.

The next morning when we returned, we learned Dad had still not slept. He'd been awake for at least fifty hours. He was increasingly restless and disoriented, though he still recognized our masked faces. A nurse had been assigned to him on a one-to-one basis because he kept removing his oxygen mask and fiddling with the oxygen machine.

We kept him company all morning, and he showed no signs of relaxing into sleep. The doctor decided to give him a dose of Aderall, and we left the hospital, hoping he'd rest if he didn't have an audience.

Twenty minutes later, the doctor called to tell me Dad had passed away. It was February 22, 2018.

Road Trip Rule # 68:

Keep calm and ramble on.

## Michigan & Illinois & Missouri:

## The New Jan Van Plan

I winterized the Jan Van in late October of 2017. The theory of winterizing is simple: drain the water lines and replace the water with RV antifreeze fluid (the kind that won't kill you if you take a sip). This prevents the water lines from freezing and breaking, which costs time and money to repair.

In practice, winterizing tends to cause anxiety, self-doubt, and bouts of knee-locking panic. It's helpful to remind yourself not to overanalyze the process. Winterizing is simpler than it sounds.

Nothing had changed with the engine—it continued to sputter when going uphill and ran smoothly otherwise. I'd taken it to a diesel mechanic in Petoskey and they poured a container of fuel treatment into the tank and told me to "let it develop". Of course, this non-repair, non-diagnostic appointment cost me over two hundred dollars.

"I'm afraid it's going to leave you stranded," said Jen. I was dropping the van off at her house for the winter because her garage doors were tall enough for it to sail through. Pulling into my own garage would have decapitated it.

"Me too, but it hasn't worsened. I might be able to get another year out of it."

The thought of driving everywhere with my fingers crossed, hoping the van would make it from Point A to Point B on a given day, wore me out. Visions of breaking down in an unfamiliar place haunted my dreams. Would I regret spending time and money on a new rig? Would I regret keeping the old one if I didn't get a new rig? One day, I tired of my obsessive if-asking. The whole problem suddenly seemed simple, as if I was focusing on the van the whole time when I should have been focusing on the experience. There was no reason to waffle.

I searched for a different Class B rig. Again, I contacted dealers and joined mailing lists and entered customized searches with email alerts.

Jen and I were discussing my search one day when Todd advised me to purchase something brand new. "Quit messing around with used stuff. You're traveling alone, and you need something reliable. Buy one with a gas engine so regular mechanics won't be afraid to work on it."

He was right—reliability should've been my top priority all along. I modified my custom searches. I studied floor plans and customer reviews and virtual walk-through tours of various rigs on YouTube. I considered gas mileage and insurance rates and trade-in values. The Dynamax Rev with the twin beds fulfilled my wishlist. It was about six feet longer and one foot wider than my original van, and had a regular entry door rather than a slider. It was manufactured by the Forest River Group, a top-quality company, and this model was touted as, "Luxury on a budget".

I watched a young couple touring a Rev at an RV show on YouTube.

Opening the side door triggered the electric entry stairs to lower. The couple stepped inside—a large television screen hung on the right directly above the two front seats, which swiveled around to provide additional seating while camping. There was no dinette. Instead, a jack-knife couch lined the wall directly behind the driver's seat and a table leg socket was positioned near the front end of the couch.

There was little counter space, but the sink was roomy and the faucet a tall household grade fixture with a sprayer. There were three propane burners (no oven) next to the sink and ample cabinet space.

The aisle narrowed in front of the refrigerator to allow more space for the bathroom, which featured generous counter space and a luxurious shower unit with an aerator-style shower head that saved water without sacrificing pressure.

In the rear end of the rig, twin beds ran along the walls. The cabinet and drawers, all household grade, were lined with cedar and featured the soft closing hardware found in contemporary kitchens. They looked nicer than the cabinets in my house.

This was a drastic upgrade from the Jan Van. I pictured myself piloting the slightly larger rig through traffic and on long stretches of highway. I saw myself making lunch at a roadside park, stowing my hiking gear, reading my book with the built-in reading light above the bed.

Before long, I located the lowest-priced dealer in the Midwest and negotiated a trade-in value over the phone. When I told him about the improvements and repairs I'd made, as well as the potential trouble with my current rig, he said, "None of that matters. We'll give you twenty thousand for it. Period, end of sentence."

On paper, it seemed I'd lost $8000 plus the hundreds I'd paid for various improvements, generator repairs, and failed diagnoses. My sister offered a different view.

"It was your trial run," said Jen. "Now you know

you like to travel that way, you learned which features you want, and at least it's still worth that much—if your transmission failed you'd be forced to invest even more money into it."

The dealer and I reached an agreement on the price, and once again I paid $1000 over the phone to reserve my new van. I'd already planned a trip to Missouri to visit friends, and if I drove through Wisconsin, I could stop at the dealer on the way. I decided to leave the antifreeze in the water lines of the old van, and I packed everything in totes for easy transfer to the new van.

I planned to spend the first night in the new rig near Starved Rock State Park, which is within an hour of the dealership and features interesting rock formations and hiking trails. I'd discovered the park when I stopped there with my daughters on a road trip in 2004, and I wanted to return.

Mother Nature had other ideas.

The day before my meeting with the RV dealer, a spring snowstorm blasted through the UP and endowed us with eighteen inches of wet, heavy snow. This came on the heels of the previous storm—the driveway, bare a mere three days before, now lay beneath two and a half feet of snow. Spring snowstorms are Mother Nature's way of testing our mettle, and mine was tattered.

I'd pulled the van out of storage so I could stock it with everything I'd need for the first road trip in the new rig. It sat in my driveway ready to roll—I just had to shovel it out. Twice. My last picture of that first van portrays a dismal scene: a white van surrounded by snow banks, including a two-foot-tall pile on the roof.

I left home at noon after the plows had cleared the roads. I drove straight through to Madison and spent the night in a hotel. I'd considered sleeping in the van, but the temperature hovered around forty, and it was supposed to drop below freezing overnight. I'd left the antifreeze in the water lines so they wouldn't freeze, but that also meant I couldn't use the bathroom or the kitchen sink.

The next morning, I sat in the lobby sipping coffee and listening to the dire predictions of the weather forecaster. Freezing rain and sleet were heading our way. Motorists were advised to stay off of the roads. The storm would arrive in three hours, and the dealership was about two hours away. If I left immediately, I'd arrive by the time they opened at 8:00 AM, two hours before my appointment. Maybe they'd fit me in to avoid the freezing rain.

I parked the van fifteen minutes before they turned on the Open sign, and approached their storefront when I saw movement behind the glass.

After I shared my concern about the weather and my planned trip to head south with my new rig, the receptionist summoned a service technician.

"Tim will walk you through your rig," said Lucy. "The only problem is, we can't pull it inside because we have other vehicles in there now that have to be finished by 10:00 AM. But you can park your old motorhome next to your new one so you can transfer your stuff more easily."

"Great idea, thank you. I'll wait here for Tim."

Lucy gestured toward the coffee and doughnuts as she answered the phone. Tim came out and introduced himself, and we walked out to the old van.

"I'll drive it around and park it next to your new one," he said.

Rain spattered the windshield.

"Oh, here it comes," said Tim. "Sounds like we're in for some hellish weather." He glanced over at me. "It's a good thing you came early."

"Have you driven the new Dynamax Rev yet?"

Tim nodded. "I drove it to the RV show in Chicago. And back."

"How does that compare to driving something this size?"

"It's not much different—the Rev is a little bigger, but you'll adjust to that quickly. And it's front wheel drive, but I'm sure you've driven those before. It drives like a minivan, if you're looking for a comparison."

He pulled into a narrow slot next to the Rev. Between the silvery needles of icy rain, it gleamed. It glowed. It looked huge—bigger than the Rolls K'Nardly—and fancy. This was no van. It was a mobile mansion. A *Van*sion.

I lost my breath for a second.

"It's bigger than I expected," I said.

"You're going to love the extra space."

Tim unlocked the door and asked if I was ready for the walk-through.

I was.

He climbed into the driver's seat. "Everything is pretty self-explanatory, but there are some interesting features. The sideview mirrors are electric—the controls are here on the door—and the rearview mirror shows the view from the camera mounted at the top of the back side of the van. It'll show you the scene back there when you hit the brakes and when you're in reverse." There was a camera on each side of the van, too, which came on with the turn signals. "No more blind spots!" He pointed out more features, and showed me how to swivel the chairs around to face the house.

"In the house," he continued, "I'll start with the control panel here by the door." He pointed to a long black panel of switches under the kitchen counter, each one labeled. He started flicking each one on and off. "Your main living area lights, your outside lights, your awning lights." He paused. "This one is for extending the awning, but the wind is coming up out there, so I don't advise you to use it right now. Don't leave the awning extended if you're not near the rig and don't leave it open overnight. If the wind comes up suddenly, it'll wrap that sucker around so fast you won't know what happened and they're extremely expensive to replace." He moved his finger to the next button. "Tank heaters. I'd turn them on if I was you, today, in this weather." He left the button on and looked at me. "You've owned RVs before, right? Oh, I guess you've got that one." He pointed to the old van. "So you already know the basics."

I nodded. "I'm familiar with filling and emptying tanks, if that's what you mean."

He straightened up and pointed to the two switches on the far left. "One's the TV antenna, one's for the inverter. If you want to run something that requires 120 volts and your house battery is sufficiently charged, you can turn on your inverter and run it. You can't run anything with a high wattage, but you could make toast or something."

He moved to the wall next to the stove and pointed at the thermostat. "This here controls your furnace, so it also controls your water heater." He turned the dial and showed me each icon, explaining what each one was as he scrolled through. "Your water heater is what they call 'on demand' which, in the RV world, means it runs through the furnace."

"The rain's getting worse," I said.

"Yes. Not the best day to be on the road." Tim pulled a remote control from a wall-mounted pocket above the thermostat. "This operates your ceiling fan. You already have a hood installed over the fan, so I'll go ahead and open it. See here,"—he showed me the screen on the remote—"you can set this thing to maintain a certain temperature. When it gets too hot, the vent will open and the fan will run until it cools down to your set temperature. Pretty slick." He turned the fan off and hung the remote back in its pocket.

"I can't hear the fan over the rain," I said.

Tim pointed at the fan. "Quietest on the market."

The entire tour was finished within ten minutes and, distracted by the weather, I had forgotten to record it. Wind whistled between the campers parked on the lot and rain pummeled the outside of my new rig. I looked around, picturing my future road trips, my artwork on the walls, my clothes stuffed into the cedar-lined drawers. Compared to my original van, it was spacious and luxurious, way more than I needed.

"You look cold," said Tim. He chuckled. "Winter just won't move out. Go ahead and transfer your stuff. Come in whenever you're ready to sign on the line."

Tim walked back inside and I ducked into the old van to transfer the totes to the new van. I shoved them on the beds, which had plastic-wrapped memory foam mattresses beneath the factory-issue bedspreads. So much for my plan to take my time and stow everything properly—it was way too cold and wet to linger without heat.

I studied the thermostat for a moment, but it already seemed foreign. I'd check the owners' manual later, I thought, when I needed to operate it. I slid into the driver's seat and swiveled it back into driving position. I could easily glance out the passenger side mirror. The steering wheel felt good in my hands.

I went inside to complete the paperwork.

I sat across from Roy, a large Humpty Dumpty of a man with a deep horizontal crease across his forehead. He rested his forearms on the desk and only moved his wrists and hands to shuffle the papers, as if his arms were too heavy to lift.

"Do you like your new rig?" He asked. He pointed to the signature line on each form as we talked. It took about fifteen minutes to sign everything and wait for the fax transmittal from my credit union, assuring the dealership they'd cover my personal check.

"I do. It's a lot larger than I expected. I knew the house was wider than the van body, but I didn't expect it to be as wide as it is. The side mirrors are great, though—my old van has car-sized mirrors."

"Do you know about the extended warranty?"

"No."

"I highly recommend it. Most people purchase it when they buy a new rig—it covers everything your vehicle warranty won't cover, and it lasts seven years."

"How does it work?"

Roy glanced at the ceiling as if he sought inspiration, even as he delivered an obviously rehearsed speech. "Let's say you have a catastrophic loss. Someone hits you or a tire blows out and wrecks your refrigerator and stove. Then you discover your furnace was affected, too. This warranty will replace all of those appliances for you, and reconstruct your walls and whatever else was ruined. Let's say you are stranded on the side of the road, sometime within the next seven years. You don't know what happened—

the motor simply stopped running. This warranty—"
he tapped the brochure— "will cover you. Just call
the number and they'll come out and tow you to the
nearest facility."

In my mind's eye, shadowy Ninja-type figures
materialized and bustled around, fixing and replacing
the torn up rig at the side of the road.

"Hmm. Sounds too good to be true."

"Well, it's expensive, but it's not so bad when you
consider it lasts seven years."

"Does it cover Canada as well? I travel there once
or twice each year."

"I believe so, yes. I can confirm that."

"What is the cost?"

"It's just under three thousand dollars. $2987."

"When do I have to decide if I want to purchase
that or not?"

He shrugged one massive shoulder. "You can call
me anytime within the next three or four days. I can
take your information over the phone if you want to
go ahead with it."

"Okay, I'll think about it for a day or two. That's a
lot of money."

"It is. But if one thing happens, it's worth it. I had
one couple in here last week who thanked me for
selling this warranty to them—their fridge quit, and it
was fully covered. Right after they had it replaced,
their furnace quit." He shook his head. "I don't know
how they got so lucky to have two faulty appliances,
but they were already three years old, so the

manufacturer's warranties had expired. They only had to pay the $100 deductible."

"Could I talk to them about their experience?"

"Sorry. That's not allowed. But if you're traveling alone—well, it's priceless. You just call the number and they'll handle everything."

Ultimately, I bought the warranty. The company had good reviews from other customers online and when I broke the cost down, it came to less than $500 per year—cheap insurance. The thought of being stranded on the side of the road, then receiving a bill for thousands of dollars, tipped me over the edge. Roy never did give me a straight answer about coverage in Canada, which I interpreted to mean the magical warranty didn't apply in foreign countries.

Roy gave me a fifty-dollar coupon to use in their store, and a new owner's kit consisting of a five-gallon bucket with a lid, a sewer hose, chemicals for the black tank, and RV toilet paper. I spent the coupon on an electrical device that plugged into an outlet to check the polarity and voltage, which I could then plug my thirty-amp cord into.

By the time I left the dealership the rain had formed a thin skim of ice on the windshield. I had virtually no memory of what Tim had said during the walk-through, but Roy had handed me an accordion file folder stuffed with owners' manuals, which I placed on the passenger seat.

I'd soon realize I should've taken the time, and perhaps even rescheduled my appointment at the dealer for a nicer day, to fully tour the motorhome and try out the different features. With the first van, I'd made the mistake of trusting everything the dealer told me; with the second one, I'd made the mistake of believing everything would work properly because it was brand new.

The weather drove me southward past Starved Rock State Park. I didn't even glance at the exit. This was not hiking weather. I decided to continue on toward my friend Kelly's place in Cape Girardeau, Missouri, where I would visit her and her family for the next few days.

I drove from freezing rain to regular rain about an hour south of the dealership. The rain gave up by the time I reached Bloomington, Illinois, and I stopped at a WalMart to get supplies and stretch my legs.

Kelly called to check on my progress.

"I left a bit earlier than planned," I told her about the weather I'd driven through. "I think I'm clear of the storm. I'm only about four hours from your place right now."

"It's only noon!" She said. "Just come a day early. I already changed the sheets on your bed."

The thought of setting up the van now seemed daunting. If I went to Kelly's early, I could set it up leisurely during my visit.

The year before, I'd parked the old van in front of her house, intending to sleep in there during my visit. Kelly was appalled.

"You're not sleeping out there on the curb," she

said. "You're sleeping in my bed. I'm bunking with the kids."

She expected me to arrive in the old van again this time—I hadn't shared my van plan in case something fell through. I texted her a photo of the new van so she'd recognize it when I pulled up out front.

Now that I'd cleared the rain, the wind became my nemesis. It pummeled me sideways with such vigor I half-expected to see a garden shed or farm animal whirl past. I took the fastest route prescribed by the GPS, over to St. Louis and then down I-55. If I kept my foot pressed to the floor, I could maintain traffic speed in the slow lane. The Vansion didn't sputter or protest, but it was disinclined to hurry.

The wind was relentless. I gripped the steering wheel and held it a quarter-turn to the right to counteract the steady blow. Every time a semi-truck passed me, the van sidled over in response to the battling air currents. I quickly became adept at safely correcting my path without jostling anything or leaving my lane.

This doesn't sound like much of an accomplishment, but I was driving a front-wheel drive Dodge Promaster 3500 with an entire house built on the back end. All of this on two axles—only four wheels. I felt a thread of panic start to wind itself through my brain and start knitting itself into a terrifying tapestry scene of the van blowing a tire. Why hadn't they built a van with dual rear wheels? Maybe I shouldn't have been trying to keep up with

Interstate traffic during a windstorm.

By the time I reached Kelly's my arms and shoulders ached from battling the wind. Her warm welcome and ready glass of wine were exactly what I needed at the end of that long day.

I first met Kelly when she was a toddler. Her parents, Kevin and Dominique, had moved to town when Kevin was hired to run the DeTour Village water department. He became my mom's boss—she worked part-time as a lab technician and operator. When we welcomed them to town, I got a new job, too: babysitting Kelly.

That first winter they spent in DeTour was one of the worst on record. Kevin shoveled a path to their front door and for me, it was like walking through a tunnel. Kevin, at over six feet tall, could peer over the top of it if he craned his neck. I visited Dominique and Kelly nearly every day after school, and sometimes I'd spend the entire weekend over there, running home (a block away) just long enough to sleep.

They lived in DeTour for about three years before moving to the western end of the UP and then to Missouri, and we kept in touch throughout the years.

Now, I visit them every year, usually on my first road trip of the season. Kelly has three kids—a son, Connor, and two daughters, Olivia and Estella.

During my stay, we browsed the bookstores, shopped the downtown area, and Kelly pointed out the Gone Girl sites (the movie was filmed in Cape

Girardeau). We hung out with her kids and her mom and cooked together and sat up late drinking wine and talking about whatever marched through our minds. We've known each other for so long I feel like I'm visiting family when I'm there.

On my second morning there, I went to the van for a change of clothes and the smoke detector beeped as if it had a dead battery. I removed the battery and it kept beeping. Smoke detectors beep at a piercing level, made exponentially worse in a small, enclosed van-sized space. The sound felt like a direct blow to my brain each time it screeched—it jangled my nerves and crossed my eyes. I wondered if locking someone in a room with a beeping smoke detector had ever been used as torture. I'd confess to just about anything to make the noise stop.

I flipped through my owner's manuals and couldn't find anything about incessant beeping. I typed the symptoms into Google and, like a good doctor, Google provided a definitive diagnosis within seconds: the house battery was low. It was connected to the smoke detector as a safety precaution to alert people before the house battery died completely. The new rigs rely on house batteries more than the old ones did—the fridge and furnace have electronic ignition systems, the toilet has an electric flush system, and of course, the lighting and the electric step that operates when you open the camper door are fed from the house battery. The panic-inducing smoke detector shriek seems like a rather drastic way to announce the fridge or furnace may not kick on.

I hauled the thick electric cord out of the side bin and plugged it into Kelly's garage with an adaptor.

The detector continued to beep for five or ten minutes (or maybe an hour) before sweet silence returned, punctuated only by birdsong. I re-inserted the battery in the smoke detector.

I had thought the brand new house battery would last longer with nothing turned on inside. I left the electronic outside step extended to conserve power, and I didn't think anything else was drawing on the battery. I later learned the radio/DVD player was hard-wired to the house battery so it wouldn't shut off. The Forest River technician I spoke to claimed this was another safety feature, but he was unable to explain what protection it offered beyond maintaining my programmed radio stations.

"I don't save radio stations on road trips," I told him. "They change every hundred miles or so."

"Hmm. I didn't think of that." He paused. "Well, it also keeps the time."

I didn't bother mentioning the time zone changes on road trips, or the way the clock on this particular DVD player lost about five minutes per week.

I stayed at Kelly's for a few more days without incident, then headed west for the next leg of my trip. I spent the first night at a KOA campground a few miles east of Kansas City, and finally set up my Vansion for the first time.

I removed the plastic from the pedestal table leg

and inserted it in the floor. The table easily fit on top and locked into place, but it was so short I couldn't squeeze my legs beneath the table when I sat on the couch. I called the dealership about this, and they were unsympathetic. They explained that table legs come in one standard length and this was an unfortunate design flaw. I later learned this wasn't true, and that someone had simply grabbed the wrong table legs off the shelf when they were outfitting the van. An oversight this basic would've been caught immediately if I hadn't been distracted by the weather at the dealership.

The memory foam mattress was as comfortable as my bed at home, and the refrigerator in my new van didn't belch and purr like the old one had. If I left the bathroom door open, it blocked the light from the hard-wired radio/DVD player. I slept like a rock.

The next day, I rose early and walked a few laps around the campground before heading into Kansas City. The Federal Reserve Bank, the Hallmark Crown Center, and Science City at Union Station were on my list of things to see. I arrived at the Federal Reserve Bank and Money Museum a few minutes before they opened, and I easily found a parking spot in the back corner of the visitors' lot. I walked the grounds of the WWI Memorial, across the street from the Fed, for a few minutes while I waited for the Fed to open.

I've wanted to tour a Federal Reserve Bank ever since I worked at a credit union as an accounting manager. Part of my job had been to order money, accept delivery from the Fed, and balance the clearing account each month, and I was curious to see the place that moved so much cash and cleared so many checks. The credit union where I worked used the Minneapolis Federal Reserve, but I figured they were all similar.

I walked into the Fed and through the security area where a friendly guard told me to enjoy my tour. The tour is self-guided with plaques and signs at each display, one of which is Harry S. Truman's coin collection. Glass panels sheltering bundled stacks of bills line the wide hallway, decorated with statistics printed on the glass: The average life span of a $1 bill is 21 months; the average life span of a $100 bill is 89 months. The tour ends at a bulletproof glass wall where you can watch three forklift-style robots named Huey, Dewey, and Louie transfer pallets of cash from one area to another. There's a small gift shop offering money-themed products including bags of shredded cash—the Kansas City office shreds over $4 million per day, according to a display sign.

From there, I walked down the sidewalk and across the street to the Hallmark Crown Center. The morning was crisp and cool and the sun warmed my face. I browsed my way through the shops until I found the Hallmark Visitor Center. The gals at the front desk welcomed me and pointed me in the direction of the displays—another self-guided tour. The Hallmark company timeline is shown, decade by decade, and Christmas ornaments from the past one hundred years are artfully balanced on pedestals. Their iconic cards are here too, in showcases illustrating the differences in artwork and fonts through the decades. Each visitor is encouraged to push the button on the bow-making machine, which creates a star-shaped bow that doubles as a souvenir.

Leaving the Visitor Center, I wandered through Crown Center and past some of the fountains for which Kansas City is known, but they weren't yet turned on for the season. Science City was across the street at Union Station, and I headed over there.

Science City encourages scientific curiosity through demonstrations and hands-on exploration. The day I was there, at least five hundred elementary students raced from exhibit to exhibit, climbing the stairs and riding the bicycles on the cables suspended at the second-story level. They screeched and chased and twirled. I threaded my way through most of the museum before admitting defeat. It was too difficult to absorb anything with such fierce interference.

Back in the van, I entered an address in Liberty, Missouri into the GPS and headed north out of the city. Kansas City had been an interesting waypoint on the way to the real reason I drove this far west: the quilt shops.

A few years before, when we were in Alaska visiting my daughter and granddaughter, I'd entered a quilt shop with a long-arm machine set up in the front room. Up to that point, I had never felt the urge to cut fabric into tiny bits and sew it back together, but something happened to me that day and a new obsession was born. After wandering through the little quilt shop and chatting with the owner, I walked outside and opened my Amazon.com shopping app on my phone and ordered a sewing machine with free-motion quilting capabilities. It was waiting for me when I returned home.

Because I had only the foggiest notion how to piece fabric together, I turned to the modern-day equivalent of a private quilting instructor: YouTube. There, I discovered Jenny Doan of the Missouri Star Quilt Company. Her videos are easy to follow and full of tips and tricks, and before long, I started calling myself a quilter.

I set up a Craft Cave in my basement and placed my new sewing machine next to the window. I bought a cutter, a mat, and piles of fabric. Special rulers, special pins, special markers. I referred to Jenny Doan as 'Aunt Jenny'. When I was ten years old, my mom taught me to sew—Aunt Jenny taught me how to quilt.

I later discovered Angela Walters, owner of Quilting is My Therapy, on YouTube. She quilts through the night, a glass of wine and a bowl of popcorn at her elbow, while her family sleeps. She's known for her intricate free-motion quilting designs and has a punchy way of talking to the camera as if you're sitting there next to her, toasting her latest design. If you need a quick shot of quilting inspiration, Angela is a good source.

When I entered Liberty, I drove once around the town square before parking down the hill from Angela's shop. The long, narrow store oozed quilting mojo. Its brick walls were lined with intricately-pieced quilts and bolts of fabrics. Long-arm quilting machines stood at the ready, some with half-finished quilts loaded and resting. A few quilters fingered the fat quarters and pondered purchasing thimbles and thread.

It was early afternoon when I left Liberty. My next stop: Hamilton, Missouri. Home of the Missouri Star Quilt Company. Mecca.

J.C. Penney's boyhood home is in Hamilton, as is his library and museum. But today, Jenny Doan puts Hamilton on the travel itineraries of thousands. Davis Street runs through the center of town and is lined with thirteen quilt shops, each one owned and operated by the Missouri Star Quilt Company. Each shop has a theme: Florals, Batik, Man's Land, Modern, etc. There's a Main Shop and a Mercantile. Around the corner, there's a workshop that offers classes, but I'd missed the latest workshop by a few days. A smattering of restaurants feature diner foods, sandwiches and barbecue. The world's largest spool of thread is here, too. Where else would it be?

The sheer abundance of fabric bolts and pre-cuts is overwhelming and I'll need to return sometime when I have a specific project in mind. I purchased a pile of random pre-cuts—at least enough to make three or four large quilts—and I had to exercise extreme willpower to leave everything else on the shelves.

Quilting and camping are linked—groups of RV Quilters post photos on Facebook and sometimes hold impromptu quilting bees in campground recreation rooms, or pull their picnic tables together outside for a quilt-along. Some motorhomes are modified for quilting. I've even seen a sewing machine bolted to a custom-built lap desk in front of the passenger seat in a Class A. I don't have enough fabric storage space in my small rig—I need something more portable for on-the-road crafting.

I stayed that night at the Eagle Ridge RV park, a privately-owned campground north of Hamilton. No eagles perched on the ridge, but I had a spectacular view of the sunset.

The next morning I realized I was driving through Madison County. I veered from the Interstate to seek the famed bridges, and found one photo-worthy structure. There were two others nearby, but they were on a gravel road—too primitive for the Vansion. I returned to the Interstate and pressed on.

By the time the Des Moines exit signs appeared I needed to stretch my legs. I left the highway and drove through West Des Moines and parked on a side street. I poked through a couple of shops before I discovered Yarn Junction, a large, bright store overflowing with colorful fiber of all kinds. The owners were preparing for Local Yarn Store day, an annual store-hopping shopping event, which started the minute they flipped on the open sign and I walked in the door.

"Welcome to LYS!" They sang out. They introduced themselves as Beth and Kate, sisters and owners of the store.

I had no idea what they were talking about and they explained everything was 20% off today only. I wandered through the store, chatting with Beth and Kate about yarn preference and favorite projects. They frequently host classes and workshops in the store and I knew this would be my favorite store if I lived within a hundred miles.

"I could use something portable for my travels," I said. "This sweater looks easy and I love the colors." I held up a sweater kit with thirteen balls of self-striping wool, all different colors.

"That is our most popular kit right now," said Beth.

"None of the skeins match, but they all magically coordinate when you knit it up," said Kate. "The only decision you have to make is which skein to grab next."

I bought the sweater kit and knitting needles and started the sweater that afternoon. It was the perfect camping project and I worked on it throughout the summer, leaving it in the van between trips and pulling it out while sitting around the campfire. By the time camping season ended, I had a new sweater.

I'd found a copy of Bill Bryson's *The Lost Continent* at a used book store and opened it that evening. It's the story of Bryson's solo road trip around the US, and it begins in his hometown—the town through which I'd driven that very morning: Des Moines, Iowa.

# Wayside Ahead:
# Power Play

When camping at a campground with electric hook-up, there's no reason to conserve power. In fact, if the temperature is on the cooler side, conserve your onboard propane by using an electric heater instead of the built-in furnace.

But if you're planning on dry camping (camping with no hook-ups) or boondocking (camping without hook-ups, in the wilderness) for several nights in a row, you'll be more comfortable if your house batteries can support your power usage.

If you're driving during the day and dry camping at night, the house batteries should charge while the vehicle engine is running, providing you with plenty of power.

If your vehicle has USB ports, plug in all USB-charged devices while you're driving so they'll be fully charged by the time you stop for the night. Most USB outlets are either directly connected to the vehicle battery or to the house battery—either way, you won't be wasting your house battery charge by plugging them in while the engine is running.

My new camper has LED lights throughout, and they use very little electricity. Even so, I have a solar lantern I use when I'm boondocking or dry camping for more than one or two nights without driving during the day. The lantern sits outside or on the dashboard during the day, then provides me with reading light in the evening.

Discover where your power leeches are—one of mine was the radio/DVD player, which didn't fully shut off. It's mounted next to the television, and the blue light kept me awake at night. I discovered it had a dedicated circuit—the fuse that fed it was not connected to anything else—so I pulled the fuse out of the panel to shut it off. This saved a small bit of power and improved my sleep. Another option would have been to install a toggle switch, but I rarely use the radio or DVD player. Pulling the fuse was the easiest solution for me.

When dry camping or boondocking, unless you run the generator, you won't have air conditioning. Keep the rig as cool as possible during the day, then open the windows and turn on the ceiling fan after the sun goes down. Two places that gather heat are the ceiling fan and the skylight. Cutting a piece of Reflectix to fit each of these openings, and securing it with Command strips, will reduce the solar effect. I also cover the ceiling fan when I'm parked in a brightly lit store parking lot for the night to keep the van as dark as possible—but only if I'm not using the fan.

One feature my van offers is the battery disconnect switch. Most newer RVs have this feature. When the battery disconnect switch is toggled, it will stop using the house battery for everything except the electronic step (and, in my case, the radio/DVD player). The step can be extended and shut off so it won't extend out every time the door opens, or you can enter through another door to avoid the step extending and burning up the battery. When the battery disconnect switch is in the disconnected position, it should still charge if you're driving or plugged into shore power (a 120-volt outlet). If the rig is new to you, verify that the house battery is charging while the engine is running.

It's important to make sure you have good voltage when you're plugged into shore power. A cheap but effective way to test the voltage is to purchase a device that plugs into a regular outlet and monitors the voltage. As a general rule of thumb, I don't run any heavy electrical loads if the voltage monitor reads lower than 112 volts (a regular voltage reading, before you have anything plugged in and running, should be 120). The one I use is called a Kill-A-Watt, P3 4460, and can be found on Amazon.com for about $35. When you plug something in and turn it on—say, a hair dryer or the microwave—you can watch the voltage on the monitor drop.

There are new smart monitors out now that communicate through an app on your smartphone, but if you're someplace without cell signal, those might not work so well.

If you frequently dry camp, it might be worthwhile to install a couple of solar panels. There are many types and sizes of solar energy systems appropriate for RVs—do your research and consult an electrician if you're considering this. My new Dynamax came with most of the solar components already installed —everything except the solar panels themselves.

MILE
2
1

# The Minnesota Creeper

The next day, I continued north toward Minnesota. Rain drizzled from clouds hanging so low the van may have cleaved their underbellies. I paused in Minneapolis long enough to sprint through Costco to stock up on supplies before heading northeast on Highway 8 toward Lindstrom, Minnesota.

The cloud-ceiling lifted by the time I glided through the quaint Swedish community. I had planned to sail through town, but the signs for

Gustaf's Up North Gallery and the Picket Fence Gals gift shop caught my eye. I browsed through both of them, soaking up inspiration from their artistic handmade products.

When I left Lindstrom I found Franconia Sculpture Park a few miles east. I drove past the large yellow sign adorned with metal bits of machinery—Big Space, Big Art—and parked in the large gravel lot. I donned my polka-dot Slogger shoes in case the ground was still wet.

The sculptures bordering the curvy garden path were made with found objects—rusty metal machine parts, discarded mirrored tiles, uprooted trees. The park itself is a nonprofit artists' organization that provides opportunities for artists to create and display their work and offers internships and residencies. It's forty-three acres of creativity and meditative bliss.

Most of the pieces were structured as abstract pinnacles or large dome-shaped screens or half-walls. An old farm shed hung from a massive swingset-style iron frame, suspended on cables at a jaunty angle as if caught mid-tornado. A rescued set of stairs climbed an interior wall section and ended six feet closer to the sky than where I stood. My favorite sculpture was built on a wheeled cart—a man-shaped collection of metal bits stood on a platform, arms akimbo as if waiting for the viewer to do something interesting. Each display caused me to see something I hadn't expected, and maybe that was the whole point.

My wending path crossed that of a young couple

discussing wedding plans as they walked. They linked hands and arms, matching their steps. I caught whispered phrases—

"...don't want more than fifty people, but your mother seems to think we should have..."

"...always wanted freesia, but if we have a winter wedding..."

"...twinkle lights. It'll be perfect."

Their words brought my own wedding to mind and my heart ached like a new bruise as I sank into the memory. We were married outside, in the local pavilion. I'd worn a beaded ivory gown and Jason was in elegant long tails with a black cummerbund. My cousin Chris walked me down the aisle toward Jason. I'm sure everyone watched our procession, though I don't recall any faces except my groom's. I'd been worried my voice would crack but I sounded strong and clear when we said our vows. We'd misplaced the flower girl's flowers and the officiant had skipped our scheduled reading and song, but it was still my favorite day and I'd do it all again if I could.

I missed Jason like an unbroken heart. Ballooning my lungs with fresh Minnesotan air, I slowly exhaled the memories and silently commanded myself to get it together.

I exited the path and crossed the parking lot to my van, thinking about dinner. Maybe I missed Jason like an empty stomach—I'd only had a few handfuls of trail mix all day. The sun occupied the sky now, having shoved the clouds somewhere beyond the horizon.

The campground I'd found on my app was only about ten minutes away, so when I entered the van through the house door I left it unlocked for this final short stretch.

A man on a motorcycle pulled off the road and flagged me down before I left the parking lot. He looked like a lame version of the middle-aged bikers in the movie Wild Hogs. I waved at him, but he flailed his arms again, and I stopped and lowered my window, acutely aware of the unlocked door.

He perched on his bike—a rather wimpy model, though it sported a Harley emblem—and removed his helmet to reveal a carefully combed, sparse head of gray hair. His jeans had sharp creases, as if they'd been ironed, and a large signet ring squeezed his right pinky. A few wiry gray hairs sprung from his chest, on full display when he unzipped his leather jacket to reveal his button-up shirt, open at the throat. If he was a superhero, his cape would've read Midlife Crisis Man.

"Can I help you?" I asked.

"I saw you walking across the parking lot just then," he said.

The hairs on the back of my neck stood up.

"My name is Phil."

"I'm Ruth," I said. I didn't know I was going to make up a name until I heard myself say it. Ruth sounded tough, though. Ruth would send this guy down the road.

"I was wondering—is your motorhome for sale?"

That sounded feeble, even to me. I was driving a brand new rig—why would it be for sale?

"No—I just bought it. It'll be for sale in about ten years." I moved the van forward a few inches.

"Wait—are you traveling alone?" He'd seen me walk across the parking lot alone, so he already knew the answer.

"I'm meeting friends."

"You're so brave." He shook his head and looked off into the distance. I glanced into the passenger side mirror to monitor the unlocked house door. Did he have a partner planning to enter the van?

I shrugged. "It's not like I travel unarmed."

He sat back slightly and adjusted his sunglasses. "Do you work on the road?"

"No, I still work a regular old job." I checked the mirror again—still no movement.

"I run a company on the internet, and I can work from anywhere. I'm thinking of buying a rig like yours. Do you like it?" His combover lifted in the breeze.

"It's fine for one person. Two would be a crush in here. Look, I've got to run." I crept forward a few more inches. My ingrained midwestern politeness battled my innate sense of self-preservation.

My inner eye saw a newspaper headline: *Geriatric Serial Killer on the Loose; He Charms, Disarms, and Leaves for Dead.*

He held up a hand. "Wait. I know this area like the back of my hand. Would you like to have a cup of coffee, and explore the Glacial Potholes?" He smiled. "They're just up the road. Coffee's on me."

Another headline: *Body Found Near Glacial Potholes.*

"No, thank you." I glanced in the side mirror again. All was clear.

"I'm not a creep," he said.

"That's what they all say." This time I continued moving and pulled out of the parking lot.

He followed me out of the sculpture park for about three miles before turning off and heading north. I didn't realize how tense I was until he turned and I noticed my shoulders were up around my ears. Another long, slow exhale and my sense of unease started to fade.

I located the Interstate State Park, on the border between Minnesota and Wisconsin, and selected a site near the center of the campground. There were two other occupied sites, and a couple strolled through the campground with their Pomeranian on a leash—a comforting illustration of normalcy.

I considered staying at the campground for the evening to avoid a second encounter with the Wild Hog wannabe, but in the end I decided not to let him ruin my plans. I grabbed my pepper spray and walked the trail from the campground to the state border and the Glacial Potholes, about 1.25 miles from my site. The path was well-traveled, but still rustic in places. I stepped over tree roots and climbed stone stairs, and inhaled the piney air. The path met the highway near the St. Croix River, and I walked across the bridge with one ear cocked for a motorcycle engine. Four bikes traversed the bridge, but none of them looked familiar.

The Glacial Potholes are natural sculptures carved by the glaciers thousands of years ago. Bowl-shaped caves and house-sized divots and boulders larger than my Vansion. The park itself has a visitors' center, and there are trails and stairways to access the potholes and see the St. Croix River from above. The rocks dwarfed me. I stood in the bottom of the Bake Oven and looked up, imagining the glacier slowly smoothing and sculpting rocks as it moved through.

Perhaps this place inspired some of the sculptors whose work I'd admired at the park.

\*\*\*

The last stop on most of my road trips is my friend Ali's house in Wausau, Wisconsin. She lives seven hours from me, and I usually spend a day or two with her before returning to reality.

I arrived in the early afternoon and we sat in her living room chatting about my trip over coffee. She looked worried when I told her about the Wild Hog wannabe.

"That makes me nervous, Jan." She took a sip of coffee, blue eyes studying me over her cup. "Do you carry a weapon?"

"Not really." I shrugged. "I have an axe."

"An axe!" Ali laughed. "I can just see you opening

your door with an axe in your hand."

"I also have a golf club." I was laughing with her now, picturing myself trying to look ominous wielding a pitching wedge. I laughed so hard I had to set my coffee down.

Ali set down her cup and straightened up, arms akimbo. "'I'm a Yooper. Don't mess with me.'" She slashed the air with an invisible axe.

"I'd probably collapse in laughter if I did that!" I brushed the laugh-tears off my face. "I might have to go for the full-on crazy act and hope that scares them away."

Eventually we stopped laughing.

"Have you thought about getting a concealed weapon permit?" She asked. "I hate the thought of you out there with all the creepers and no firearms."

"The guys at work say the same thing." I took a sip of coffee. "They all think I should be packing heat, even when I take a walk in the woods."

"And you don't think so?"

"I don't want to worry about that, or even think about it. Loading a gun, unloading it, checking it all the time, thinking about where it's pointed, where it's stored, and the border crossings—another hassle." I shrugged. "There's no easy answer."

"You're a brave one." She smiled. "You're a Yooper, so you're not scared."

# Wayside Ahead:
# Safety & Security

Most people, when they discover I travel alone, respond the way Ali did: "you're brave". They ask about weapons, tactics, and strategies to avoid attack. Sometimes they offer suggestions.

"Get an old pair of men's boots and set them outside the door."

"Make campground reservations in a man's name —and tell them there are two of you."

"Keep a loaded shotgun inside the door of your camper."

"Take self-defense classes."

"Put a cardboard cutout in the passenger seat." (This one's my favorite.)

The trouble with most of these suggestions is, they assume other campers won't see through the flimsy props and deduce, correctly, that I'm alone. They'll also deduce that I'm paranoid.

When I pull into a campground and park in a campsite, everyone knows I'm traveling solo before I exit the van. Not only am I driving, no one is sitting in the passenger seat.

Most campgrounds have a speed limit of five miles

per hour, and most campers stop whatever they're doing to watch new rigs pull in and set up. There isn't much to do at a campground, and we all love to critique the parking technique and picnic table placement of new arrivals.

My security strategies are few: I remain aware of my surroundings and I carry pepper spray when I go hiking or biking. If I pull into a place that doesn't feel safe, I leave. And I'm prepared to drive away, even if I'm set up and connected to utilities, if I feel threatened. I'll happily sacrifice my electric cord, water hose, and sewer hose if necessary.

Once, I left a campground just minutes after parking in my site. The site itself was so narrow I felt like I was encroaching on the family next to me. The man on my other side was sitting under his awning, watching my every move through half-closed eyes while I plugged in.

"You did a purt' good job backin' that thing in," he said.

I glanced over to take in his baggy shorts and fishing hat, beer in hand and surly expression.

"Thank you." I pulled my electric cord out of the bin and unreeled it.

"Is a nice skirt you got on." He belched.

The campground was packed and chaotic. Kids were screaming and racing around on bikes and on foot. People were cooking on their grills and yelling at each other. It was a hundred degrees in the shade with no breeze.

And Creepy McBeerson kept talking.

"Virginia!" He yelled into his camper door. "Git me a beer!"

"For Chrissakes, Harvey." Three seconds later, an arm shot out of the camper and dropped a beer into Harvey's hand.

His eyes never left me as he opened his fresh beer and rested it on his bullfrog belly.

I watched him from the corner of my eye and grabbed my phone as if it had just rung. I hit the button to silence it, in case someone really called, and held it up to my ear. For some reason, I didn't want to hurt Harvey's feelings but I knew if I stayed at this campground I'd spend my evening inside to avoid further interactions. The charade felt silly and weak, but it seemed easier than simply saying I'd changed my mind.

"Hello?" I spoke into the phone.

"Are you kidding me?" I said. I rolled my eyes at Harvey. "No, I just set up." Pause. "Okay. I'm on my way."

"You leavin' so soon?" He took a swig of his beer.

"Not soon enough," I muttered under my breath.

# CIRCUITOUS
# ROUTES

Road Trip Rule # 49:

Every route is a scenic route.

# Indiana: RV Conference

Owners of Forest River brand motorhomes receive a complimentary membership in FROG—a cheesy acronym for Forest River Owners' Group—which includes access to private online forums where owners can network and learn more about their campers. Every year there are several FROG Rallies around the country, where owners of new Forest River brand RVs (less than three years old), are entitled to free repairs for minor defects.

I attended the rally in Goshen, Indiana, four months after I purchased my Dynamax Rev. The rally application allowed three requested repairs or issues, and I listed the following:

1. Both pedestal table legs are too short—they are 24" and should be at least 29".

2. The trim near the rear back-up camera is bubbled.

3. The trim above the driver's and passenger's seats (below the television) is crooked and won't stay in place.

My list of paltry repairs stared back at me and I thought about the different houses I'd rented and owned. When I first left home at seventeen, I lived in my car for a week before finding a ramshackle one bedroom apartment with walls so thin we could hear the neighbors chew. Ed and I lived in places with sloping floors, drafty windows, recalcitrant furnaces, and uneven stairs. Later, with Jason, we designed and built a house together. Most recently, I bought a house for myself that required major renovations, some of which still aren't done.

*How lucky am I*, I thought, *to own a brand new Vansion? How did this even happen?*

The rally promised five days packed with seminars, factory tours, and social events with the other owners. It included some meals and a parking space with electric and water hook-up, and one free dump service during the week. The rally itself wasn't free— it cost $425 for a member to enjoy these benefits.

I arrived at the rally shortly after 8am. Parking attendants waved flags to indicate where I should drive and I pulled up to the end of a line of motorhomes.

A man with a clipboard stepped up to my window. "How long is your rig?"

"Twenty-five feet," I answered.

"We assign spaces according to length," he said, scanning his list of vacant sites. He wrote my site address on a piece of paper, tucked it under my windshield wiper, and told me to pull forward.

A jolly man with a bristly gray mustache and a large straw hat drove up on a golf cart, grabbed my site number, and led me through the fairgrounds. My site was on a dirt road north of the horse racetrack.

He gestured toward the site and pulled over to direct me as I backed in. The site he indicated sank off the side of the road onto reddish clay about a foot lower than the road. Soft and damp. When I was ready to pull out in five days, I'd have to drive back up the slope to exit. This would pose a problem with my front-wheel drive and heavy back end. The other side of the road looked like sandy soil and patchy grass. High and dry.

I lowered my window. "That site looks a bit low—can I have one across the street there?"

"It'll be fine." He adjusted his hat. "We can bring you some boards to park on, if that helps."

"I have front wheel drive and most of the weight is in the back. The wheels sometimes spin on dry pavement on inclines like this."

He shrugged. "You won't have a problem."

He guided me in, lining me up with the rig behind me and stopping me when I was twelve inches from it. When my next-door neighbor arrived a couple of hours later, he requested a site across the road and was immediately ushered to the spot I'd requested. I asked to be moved again and was dismissed with a wave of the hand.

I couldn't help but wonder: if I'd been a man, would they have granted my request to park in the higher lots? There were several open sites there, and they remained open all week long.

The RVs were parked according to more than length—the fairgrounds resembled a suburban neighborhood with strict zoning laws. The Class A motorhomes (upper class, mostly retired couples with a dog or two) were arranged by model name and parked in neat rows a few streets over from the R-Pod village (younger couples, fewer pets, party atmosphere) and there were two full streets of Class C Sunseekers (upwardly mobile middle class, with kids and/or dogs). The Class C Forester models formed a thicket in the northeast corner of the 'town', on the edge of which sat my very own Vansion.

The first scheduled event was dinner on opening night, in the large tent on the west side of the fairgrounds. Mass-prepared dinners are usually meat-centric with sides of corn and potatoes, none of which are on my regular diet, but I attended so I could meet a few people and hear the announcements. Hundreds of campers were fed in a quick and orderly fashion while the FROG Rally Master of Ceremonies entertained us with a welcome speech that promised in-depth RV education during the next five days, with plenty of social activities sprinkled throughout the schedule. I sat between a couple from Iowa who'd never attended a rally before, and a couple from Ohio who said this was their eighth FROG Rally, even though they drove a twelve-year-old Class A and weren't eligible for any free repairs.

On my way home from dinner, one of the golf carts whizzing around stopped next to me. The driver, a woman with long salt-and-pepper hair and a FROG Rally Volunteer T-shirt, waved me over.

"Would you like a tour of the grounds?"

"That sounds fun, thanks!"

I sat next to her and we careened down the street. We drove past each of the "neighborhoods" I'd noticed earlier, and she told me she was part of the volunteer staff that worked for a discount on the week-long stay

"It's tons of fun," she said. "I've basically been driving around in circles all afternoon. Each of us only have to volunteer for a few hours. I'm Lois, by the way." She pointed to a building on our left. "That's the main FROG office for the week—they handle pretty much everything. Start there if you have a problem or want information about Goshen."

She steered around a family of four with ice cream cones and veered over to avoid colliding with another golf cart. I gripped the thin bar below the windshield, half-expecting it to come off in my hand.

"This might be the most fun I've ever had in a golf cart," I told her.

She laughed. "I was raised to drive it like I stole it, no matter what it is. That's my favorite little walkway." She pointed to a sidewalk connecting two streets. Someone had planted flowers in old handbags and arranged them in little garden-themed vignettes along the walkway. "They're so creative with their plants." She gestured toward a fence with a sign reading "Jean-etically Modified Plants", where several flowers were planted in old blue jeans that stood upright in cowboy boots. When I walked by later I realized the belt loops were tethered to the fence posts.

Lois cranked the wheel and we cruised onto a narrow street I hadn't noticed earlier. "I'll show you the secret neighborhood."

We rolled past a dozen Class A motorhomes, each of them parked with their awnings extended over their patio areas. Chairs were arranged at each site but I didn't see any people. We were on the west border of the fairgrounds, behind the dinner tent, in a separate subdivision accessible only by this alleyway and one other street, on which we exited after Lois looped around the few sites. I told her where my site was, and we zoomed back to my corner of the campground.

It wasn't until I'd sipped my nightly cup of herbal tea and brushed my teeth that I realized Lois hadn't asked me if I was traveling alone. Maybe she was traveling alone, too.

The next morning, I felt a bit upside down when I woke up. It had rained during the night and softened the ground, and the rear tires had sunk about four inches into the soft earth. The van was now eight inches higher in the front than it was in the rear. I stopped by the customer service office on my morning walk to tell them about my concerns and asked to be relocated. They assured me, without looking at it, that my parking area was perfectly fine and the chances of my not being able to pull out of there in a front-wheel drive vehicle were "practically nil".

I attended two seminars during the first full day: RV Electrical Systems in the morning and Generator Maintenance in the afternoon.

There were bowls of free fuses on a side table, and one lucky soul won an RV surge protector as a door prize. RV electrical systems aren't as complex as they seem at first glance. It's easy to get confused because there are two different voltages, and this tends to overwhelm some owners. As you use your RV more and more, you'll become comfortable with the electrical system. The electric seminars at the rally were presented by Mike Sokol, who began his career in the 1970s as an OSHA instructor. He taught Dolby how to install surround sound, and he operated sound systems for AC/DC, Beyoncè, and a few others. He has a website, rvelectricity.com, and he writes newsletter articles for rvtravel.com.

Mike talked about voltage monitors, how converters work, and maintaining batteries. There were about eighty of us in attendance, most of us dutifully transcribing Mike's lecture.

The generator seminar focused on maintenance. My favorite tip from the afternoon was to take a photo of the generator nameplate and keep it in the owner's manual in case you need the model or serial number. The generator on my rig is between the back wheels—I have to shimmy underneath the van to access it while visions of the Rolls K'Nardly dance in my head. I didn't discover this design flaw until the generator stopped working and I had to press the reset button.

The factory tour was scheduled on day two. Nine of us boarded a bus in the morning and traveled about twenty minutes to the Elkhart, Indiana plant where we walked through the manufacturing area of the Forest River Galleria/Cross Fit Class B vans. They were the same size as my original van, on a Mercedes chassis. One woman asked the question I'd been wondering about: How can we get a copy of the electrical schematic for our rigs?

"There is no such thing," said Adrian, our tour guide. He resembled a young Charlie Sheen and pushed his mirrored shades up on his forehead when we entered the building. "We give the technicians a blueprint showing where we want the outlets and other electrical components installed, and they determine the rest as they're building them in. It's quite possible that five vans, built the same week, won't have the same wiring schemes. One tech might take the wires overhead, for instance, and the next one will feed everything through the walls."

"Well, how do we know where we can drive a nail?" Asked Tammy. She was a first-timer, here from Kansas with her husband Dave, dressed in matching blue shirts that read "It's five o'clock somewhere". Dave was unimpressed with the tour; Tammy was nearly hostile. The humidity had frizzed her hair and she looked overheated. Whether that was an effect of the heat or her own indignant attitude, I wasn't sure.

"I don't recommend you drive a nail anywhere," said Adrian. "Use Command hooks."

Adrian approached the first van in the tour, which was in the beginning stages of conversion. Adrian maintained a steady commentary as we looked inside each vehicle. He said they turned out three units per day at this shop.

We walked through the facility and observed five vans, each at a different stage of completion, then toured a finished one in the parking lot.

"Any questions?" Adrian asked. He looked at each of us except Tammy.

"I noticed each van has a wet bathroom," I said. "Any plans to return to the dry bathroom design?"

"Yes! One of the 2019 models will have a dry bathroom." Adrian looked around expectantly for more questions.

"I also noticed the vans are set up for two people —larger beds, dinette with two seats—and there's a growing trend right now for solo travelers, like me. Any plans to offer designs for solo travelers? Or, better yet, any plans for modular designs so the owner could pick and choose which features she wants and order a semi-custom rig?" The list of features on my fantasy van included an outside storage drawer for my bicycle, more electric outlets, a comfortable chair with a fold-out table/desk or work station, a smaller fridge and freezer, two burners rather than three, and the option to replace the passenger seat with shoe storage cubbies.

He gave me his Hollywood grin. "You've got big ideas. There aren't enough solo female travelers to warrant a separate design. We just don't have enough interest. As for the modular design, that's a great idea. I might work on that one."

"There might be more interest if you had more solo-friendly designs," I said. "There are thousands of solo females—there are more of us than you might think."

"But they won't listen to their own customers, so they'll never find out," said Tammy. She shook her head and walked toward the bus. The tour was over.

When we returned, about fifty brand new rigs were parked at the fairgrounds for rally attendants to tour.

An entire sales lot had popped up with rows of Class A motorhomes, Class B and C units, and tow-behind campers. Salespeople milled about like fishermen monitoring their bait, waiting for one of us to bite.

The Class A diesel pushers were by far the most elegant. Many featured a washer and dryer and a master bathroom with two sinks and—my favorite feature—a heated faux marble floor. I'd never understood the reason for two sinks in a household bathroom, let alone a camper bathroom. One rig had an additional half-bath off the living room.

"I don't know about you," the woman standing next to me in the Class A said, "but I don't want to clean more than one bathroom when I'm on vacation."

I agreed.

It was easy to forget I was in a house on wheels. These motorhomes were more luxurious than any home I'd ever dreamed of owning.

The next day, Wednesday, the scheduled seminars didn't appeal to me. Another rainstorm had moved through, leaving a clean, cool morning. A good day for a bike ride.

Goshen, population around 30,000, is in the heart of Amish country. The fairgrounds are on the eastern edge of town and easily accessible via the Abshire Park Trail, which begins across the street from the fairgrounds and meanders through a lovely wooded area. It connects with the Pumpkinvine Nature Trail, which crosses Lincoln Avenue before becoming the

Maple City Greenway.

I followed the trail most of the way to the Old Bag Factory, a large brick building originally used to manufacture laundry soap, bath soap, and toilet paper, later sold to the Chicago Detroit Bag Company. It became one of the company's leading producers of bags until it went out of business in 1982. Today, the facility hosts a restaurant and several stores, and I browsed my way through everything before pedaling downtown.

I continued on the bike path through town and across the Elkhart River, then popped out on Third Street where I found a bike stanchion and chained my bike to it. My first downtown stop was Reverie, a yarn store in an old building with high ceilings and piles of colorful fiber. From there, I wandered to Found, a store that features artwork and goods from around the globe as well as a basement full of antiques. The clerk was chatty.

"Is this your first time in Goshen?" She straightened up the check-out area while she talked.

"Yes—I'm camping at the fairgrounds east of town." I set my rooibos tea on the counter.

"Oh!" She clasped her hands. "The FROG Rally?"

I nodded.

"I forgot that was this week. It's been so hot and humid, nobody's moving much. If you brought your bicycle, you should check out our bike trails."

"I'm doing that today." I smiled.

"Have you had lunch yet?"

I hadn't.

She handed my change and the small bag of tea to me.

"Try the Maple Indian Cuisine, just up the block and across the street." She pointed north. "They're fast and delicious, and their prices are reasonable."

She was right—the waitress at the Maple Indian Cuisine seated me near the window where I could watch passersby while I ate the shrimp masala, which she delivered within moments. It was dark and quiet inside, and it felt good to rest my legs for a little while. I was in the diner for less than thirty minutes.

I walked a few blocks north and found Shirley's Gourmet Popcorn Company.

"Welcome to Shirley's!" A young woman called out when I entered. "It's a great day for popcorn!" Her energy was contagious and I smiled back at her. Two others were behind the counter with her, bantering about which popcorn flavors they liked best.

"Hello, there," I said. "I'm looking for something not too sweet."

"How about some Chicago style? It's cheese popcorn and caramel corn mixed together. It's our most popular blend."

I scanned the menu on the wall. They had my favorite.

"I'll take the white cheddar."

Next, I walked a few blocks south until I came to the Maple City Market, a small organic grocery store. I stocked up on fruit and yogurt and homemade granola before heading back to my bike.

The last full day of the rally, Thursday, most of the seminars were presented by salespeople. I attended one related to tire maintenance that featured an add-on tire pressure monitoring system. If any of us purchased a set immediately, they would install the system for free. Another one touted the benefits of solar panels and offered to install them for free. I wandered in and out of several seminars that morning, then returned to the van for lunch and to await the repair technicians.

Two Forest River technicians arrived shortly after lunch and quickly installed additional screws on the outside of the camper where the trim had bubbled up, and inside where the trim seemed as if it had been cut too long to fit properly. They looked at my pedestal table legs and promptly exchanged them for longer ones. It felt so comfortable to be able to sit at the table, after sitting next to it for four months.

"There's one more thing," I told them. "It happened on the way here. The outside temperature sensor is registering random readings—it said 39 degrees for a while, then switched to 104 degrees, then back to a colder temperature again."

Andy, the technician, shrugged. His jeans hung on his hip bones and he hiked them up with one thumb. "You'll have to go to a Dodge dealer for that. There's one nearby, if you want the number."

"No, I'll handle it when I get home. Thanks for everything else, though—it looks much better, and I can actually use the table now."

During the week I'd made friends with the folks in the camper across from me—Dale and Ellen, from Maryland, who had been married, divorced, and married each other again. We developed a habit of meeting up each evening to compare notes on the seminars and tours we'd attended during the day. I wandered over to their site in the late afternoon on the last day.

"You going to dinner tonight?" Dale asked as I approached. He gestured to an empty chair and I sat down next to him.

"No. It's nice of them to provide meals, but it's not really my kind of food."

"You a vegetarian or something?"

I grinned at him. I loved his direct, politically semi-incorrect delivery. "Yes."

"I have a niece who's vegetarian. She was always different." He sipped his beer and gazed off into the distance. "She's the weird one of the family."

Ellen's silhouette appeared in the doorway. "You givin' her a hard time, Dale?"

"No, no. Just talkin' about Amber and her weirdness."

"I'm a vegetarian," I explained.

"Oh, lord. Dale can't handle anything that progressive." Ellen opened the door and carried a glass of wine and cheese tray down the stairs. "Care for a bite? Where's your wine glass?"

I grabbed my glass and a chair while she settled in

next to Dale.

"Where did you guys go today?" I asked. I plopped my chair down across from them, my back to the sun, and helped myself to a slice of cheese.

"We toured a car museum," said Ellen. She nodded toward Dale. "His bucket list, not mine."

"Oh, Jesus, woman." Dale gritted his teeth. His mustache hid most of his mouth—I could barely see the downturned corners. "And how many goddamned garden shows have we attended? And how many—what are those—yarn stores have we shopped?"

"I know, I know. Just sayin'." Ellen rolled her eyes at me.

"Was the car museum all you'd hoped?" I asked Dale.

He suddenly looked rapt. "There's a red Volkswagen bug there, with an iridescent paint that's—" He placed his hand on his heart and sighed. "I just love it. There are no words."

"It was a religious experience," Ellen deadpanned.

We said our goodbyes and exchanged email addresses, and wished each other happy and safe travels. I planned to leave early the next morning. I was eager to return home and visit with my Aunt Karen, who'd just arrived on her annual road trip from Alaska. She was already parked in Jen's yard.

\*\*\*

I rose the next morning at 4:45 AM, made coffee,

unplugged, and started the van. I pressed the gas but the tires didn't catch. They churned rich reddish-brown clay and grass into a farm-style tangle. I tried reverse, mindful of the minuscule twelve-inch margin between my rear bumper and the rig behind me, but that didn't work either.

This was no surprise, considering I'd expected this very scenario when I first spied the slope down into the campsite. Why hadn't I insisted they relocate me? And why hadn't I tried to leave the night before, when others would have been around to assist?

Stewing was unproductive. I cleaned the van, wiped down all surfaces and mopped the floor, then speed-walked around the grounds with my flashlight trained on the path ahead.

I waited for the maintenance workers to arrive at 7:00, and found a couple of them milling around in the garage. I introduced myself to the nearest one.

"Kenny," he said, hand extended. "What can I do for you?"

"I'm in a bit of a pickle. My rig is stuck. It's front wheel drive, and the back tires have sunk into the earth."

"Have you tried to pull out?" He gulped coffee from a travel mug and wiped his mouth with the back of his hand.

"Yes—the wheels just spin."

"And what kind of rig is it?"

"It's a Dynamax Rev. Class B-Plus. Dodge chassis."

"Huh. Front wheel drive. " He scratched his jaw.

"That's—hey, Brent! We've got a situation."

Brent walked over and we explained everything.

"Let's grab a cart and get over there—see what we need. Charlie can bring the tractor." He turned to me. "Don't worry, we'll get you out of this."

Charlie, about four and a half feet tall, overheard us and climbed onto the tractor. Brent, Kenny and I boarded a golf cart and led Charlie to my site.

They scratched their chins, walked a few circuits around the van, then Charlie and Kenny stood aside while Brent started the van and tried to drive it out. The front tires churned the clay. Nothing else moved.

"Oh, boy. They should have parked you over there." Kenny nodded across the road.

"I asked to park over there, but they said I'd be fine here," I said.

"I guess the rain didn't do you any favors, but you should've been placed on one of the higher sites."

Kenny left, then returned with some slabs of wood. He laid them in front of the tires and tried driving out again, but the tires wouldn't grab them. He and Brent pushed while Charlie drove. Nothing worked.

"We can't hook onto the front of this thing without damaging it," said Kenny. "Who's he talking to?"

Brent was on the phone.

"Corporate," said Charlie.

Brent stuffed the phone back into his pocket and paced back and forth again. He looked at the van's front bumper and pried a small plastic piece out of it.

"Anything I can do?" I asked.

"We'll need a bolt that threads into this—" He pointed. "And we should be able to hook onto the bolt. But we have to pull you straight out—if we pull at an angle, we'll break something."

The road was narrow—pulling the van straight forward, with a tractor, might not even put the front wheels on the pavement. Kenny asked the neighbors across the street to move their truck so the tractor would have a few more feet in which to maneuver.

I opened my storage bin and located the tire changing kit, which also held the magic eye bolt Brent needed. He threaded it into the nut embedded in the front bumper and hooked a rope from the tractor to the eye bolt.

Brent started the van again while Charlie drove the tractor forward gently, in as straight a line as he could manage, and the van floated up out of the muck and onto the road. Kenny and I whooped and clapped, and a few of the neighbors cheered along with us.

I thanked the three guys and wished them well, and pulled out of the fairgrounds exactly three hours later than I'd planned. About fifty of the nearby campers had emerged from their RVs to line up on the street and wave good-bye. I held my coffee cup aloft in a friendly salute, a one-woman parade.

Twenty miles down the road, the outside temperature read-out stopped registering. Then the air conditioner quit.

Road Trip Rule # 38:

It's okay to eat s'mores for dinner.

MILE
2
3

## Repairs

The air conditioner was kaput. The only way to cool the interior of the van was to run the house air conditioner, which required the generator. I used it sparingly to conserve propane.

The outside temperature sensor didn't heal itself, either. I didn't realize they were linked.

I also suspected the compass on the dash didn't work. The owner's manual directed me to drive around in circles to calibrate the compass, but after several dizzying attempts, the compass refused to register. It wasn't an issue until one foggy day when I was driving in an unfamiliar area and my GPS directed me down a two-track road. It felt like the wrong direction, but I had no real proof—the corner of the GPS screen that usually displays the direction of travel showed a dash mark. It had lost its way. I finally shut it off for a few seconds and when I turned it on again, the GPS graciously recalculated and sent me down a lovely paved highway. This pleased my internal compass, but I still wanted to fix the one on the dashboard.

Because the air conditioner, temperature sensor, and compass were all part of the original chassis, and not part of the Forest River/REV modifications, I needed to find a Dodge Promaster dealer for repairs —many Dodge dealers aren't Promaster dealers. The two closest to my home base are each three hours away—one is on the west side of the state in Traverse City, and one is on the east side in Alpena. I'd never been to Alpena, and decided the needed repairs were a good excuse to explore the area.

Alpena is a picturesque town on lower Michigan's northeast coast—a great place to camp during repair trips. I arrived in town the evening before my first appointment and stayed in the Walmart parking lot with two other campers stationed at the far reaches of the blacktop. I arose before daybreak and drove to Island Park where I made coffee and read. Island Park, owned by the City of Alpena, is a seventeen-acre park in the Thunder Bay River. At sunrise, I crossed the pedestrian bridge and explored some of the trails that crisscross the island. There are several fishing platforms and a few sets of stairs, and the paths travel from low ground near the water to higher ground among trees. I encountered two other women, three deer, and a rabbit.

There are a couple of other parks downtown on Lake Huron, and a few blocks of shops and restaurants, but my favorite feature of Alpena is the bike path. From the dealership, I pedaled to the Alpena Bi-Path trailhead near Carter Street, on the south shore of the Thunder Bay River. I followed the river for a little way before crossing the bridge and wending my way around Besser Lake, then circled around the Alpena Wildlife Sanctuary (which includes Island Park) before crossing the river again. The farmers' market was set up at Mich-e-ke-wis Park and I returned to the dealership with a brimming bike basket of vegetables.

The mechanic quickly ascertained that my ambient temperature sensor, located on the driver's side mirror, was defunct. That sensor controlled the vehicle air conditioner, which explained why the van refused to provide cool air. The parts had to be ordered, which took about a week. The repair required a second visit after the parts arrived, but at least it was covered under warranty.

The compass was another story. Evidently, a Forest River technician had cut the compass wire when he installed the new motorhome roof that extends out over the van cab. I contacted Forest River through their website and, after several emails and phone calls back and forth with a manager, he said if I sent him a copy of the paid receipt he'd mail me a check to cover it. This was the first time he'd heard of any such problem.

Forest River honored their word: I received a check in the mail within a month of the repair. The compass direction is now displayed on the dashboard screen. At any given time, this is either a comforting confirmation or a reason to pull over and reassess my route.

# Wayside Ahead:
# A Few Words On Parking

My strategy for parking in cities has evolved a bit since I purchased the first van. It was narrower and shorter in length than my new rig, and easier to fit into parking spaces. In cities that offer parallel parking on the street, I would try to find a spot at one end of the block so I wouldn't get trapped between two other cars, and I could take up the entire space without trapping someone else. The van extended about one inch past each of the parking lines.

Parking garages are not an option as they are too low, and many surface parking lots aren't an option because you're not allowed to take up two spaces.

In my new Class B, which is twenty-five feet long and eight feet wide, I can still fit into parallel parking spaces but I need two of them.

If I have time to plan my city visit, I check Google Maps and see if cars are parked along the streets. I look for street parking one or two streets off the main drag, where the cars are moving slower and they have time to navigate around my boxy vehicle. If there are parking meters, I simply straddle two parking spaces and pay for both meters.

One issue with parking along a city street is the

height of the camper and the signposts at the edge of the sidewalk. My awning is attached to the passenger side of the vehicle, and it sticks out a few inches farther than my sidewall. I noticed, as I glided into a parallel parking spot, the signpost was mere inches from the edge of the curb. When I adjusted my passenger side mirror to view the awning, I realized the sign was at the perfect height to snag the awning. This is something we don't encounter when parking a regular vehicle and I wouldn't recommend backing into a parallel spot for this reason, unless you have someone spotting you from the sidewalk.

I also look for parking lots on Google Maps and try to determine whether or not I'd be able to park in one of the downtown lots. Grocery stores, libraries, parks, and churches might have large enough parking lots for me to use without inconveniencing others. When I use store parking lots, I go in and buy a few things to support the store. If I park at a library, park, or church, I look for signs to make sure they don't prohibit parking and if the lot is more than half full, I leave the remaining spaces open for others.

When I park in a parking lot, I try to back into a space at the edge of the lot that will allow me to pull out without making any tight turns. If the lot fills up while I'm out exploring, I'll still be able to exit easily. Also, I can take up one parking spot this way because when I back up to align the rear tires with the curb or edge, the rear end of the rig will extend out beyond the parking lot (assuming there are no bushes or obstacles in the way).

Before entering any parking lot, pay attention to the angle of the approach. Once you're familiar with your particular rig, you'll be able to gauge with some accuracy whether or not the bottom of the rig will scrape when you drive up a ramp. If you're not sure, proceed slowly or find someplace else to park.

Road Trip Rule # 72:

Paper maps trump GPS.

## GPS Management

I grew up with paper maps. Poring over the atlas on the kitchen table while Mom cooked dinner, I'd seek out scenic routes, curvy rivers, and towns with interesting names. Estimating the distance from point to point with an index card marked to match the map scale granted the trip a level of reality and depth. Discovering two towns with the same name, especially if one of them was well-known and the other obscure, sped up my heart rate.

"Can you imagine someone traveling to Denver, and ending up in Denver, Missouri instead of Denver, Colorado?"

"I've never heard of Denver, Missouri," said Mom. She was making gingered carrots, chopping while she talked.

"That's because—" I flipped to the index at the back, found the Missouri column, and ran my finger down city names. "Denver, Missouri has a population of 74. It's smaller than DeTour!"

"Hopefully your traveler would figure out they made a wrong turn." She dumped the carrots into the skillet and stirred them around. The smell of butter and fresh grated ginger permeated the kitchen.

"The two Denvers are about 625 miles apart. I wonder if Denver, Missouri even has a gas station."

Mom set a stack of plates next to the atlas. "Time to set the table. You'll have to move your travel business into the other room."

I was in my mid-thirties by the time I owned a GPS, and it seemed a marvel of invention. Entering any street address in the USA or Canada quickly produced a route, complete with an estimated time of arrival. The screen was tiny and the graphics were poor, but none of that mattered because the patient woman who lived inside the device guided me through each turn and recalculated without complaint.

One major drawback of the GPS, then and now, is the tiny worldview it offers. It only has a few route options, and sometimes none of them are acceptable. I sometimes add waypoints on the GPS to force it to take me along a specific route or turn the volume off and head in the general direction of my target, and let the GPS perform its incessant recalculations in silence.

Now, when I travel in the Vansion, I shut off the tolls option on the GPS so it doesn't include turnpikes. I'd rather poke along on a two-lane road and see more interesting things. The one trouble with this option, for me, is that when I'm south or east of Michigan, I need to remember to turn the tolls option back on when I'm ready to head home, or the GPS will route me through Wisconsin to avoid the toll at the Mackinac Bridge. The toll option also needs to be activated to enter or exit Canada.

Tolls aren't the only navigation nemeses.

When I revisited Maine in 2018, I spent one night in a Walmart parking lot west of Rochester, New York. The next morning, I programmed a Burlington, Vermont address into the GPS, and added a couple of waypoints I'd discovered—Chimney Bluffs State Park, and The Wild Center, near Tupper Lake.

I walked the beach at Chimney Bluffs at daybreak, coffee cup in hand. Lake Erie lapped at my feet, so calm it was difficult to imagine the powerful blasts of wind and water that had carved the sandstone chimneys looming like sentinels along the shore. Signs peppered the beach advising hikers to stay off the hazardous sandstone formations. Judging from the footprints, not many heeded the warnings.

From there, I drove a scenic route (according to the atlas) to The Wild Center, a park that occupies 115 acres in the Adirondack Mountains and features an intricate, elevated trail with stunning views and several activities. If you've ever wondered what it's like to sit in an eagle's nest, you can climb into the human-sized nest at the apex of the elevated trail and experience it for yourself. Trails loop and wind around native animal exhibits and through the iForest, an immersive sound experience designed to intensify the short hike through the curving trails in that section of the park.

When I left The Wild Center in the late afternoon, I was about a hundred miles from Burlington, and the GPS directed me along Highway 3 to Highway 9N, through Saranac Lake and Lake Placid. I enjoyed the drive, a beautifully winding road through tall evergreens with small towns interrupting the flow every now and then. The traffic was light, the sun bright, and the driving easy.

Until I encountered the Essex ferry.

It was a small ferry with an overhead framework perfectly positioned to peel the lid off the van. Taking it was out of the question.

I checked the settings on the GPS. Sure enough, I'd forgotten to turn off the ferry option. I updated the GPS and learned I was 65 miles by road—not 17 —from my destination. There is another ferry across Lake Champlain from Plattsburgh, New York, to

Burlington, Vermont. I could have driven north from Essex and taken that ferry, which, according to the website, was large enough to accommodate my rig. However, I was afraid I'd bottom-out while driving on or off the ferry, so I chose to drive around the lake instead. As I drove around the southern tip of Lake Champlain, the sun sparkled on the water, illuminating the boats with a golden glow as it dropped ever lower and finally disappeared behind the mountains.

By the time I reached South Burlington it was past 9:00 PM and getting dark. I glided into a parking spot at Walmart and settled in for the night. There were six other rigs parked nearby—four towable campers and two large Class A diesel pushers. My Class B+ brought diversity to the group.

To avoid another such unintended detour, I now study the atlas and determine which route I'd like to take. I make note of the towns I'll pass through, and if there's time, I search for shops, events, and interesting sights along the route. When I program the destination address into the GPS, I enter one or two waypoints to the route. I also review the route on the tiny GPS screen to make sure I'm not hitting an Interstate or some other road I want to avoid. My new GPS allows me to avoid a specific road after entering the destination, and I sometimes use that feature as well. If you don't have an atlas, you can do this on Google Maps or some other electronic mapping software that allows you to choose the route.

Most of the time, after I enter the items I'd like to avoid (ferries, tolls, U-turns, unpaved roads) if I choose the shortest route rather than the fastest route, the GPS guides me on a logical route without Interstates.

Another issue with the GPS is its lack of information regarding bridge clearances. My current rig is 11'2", so I won't go under anything that's less than 11'10" high, since things can move and shift over the years. There are GPS units on the market that include bridge clearances—you can program your rig's height, or the lowest height you're willing to squeeze under, into the GPS and it will produce a route avoiding those too-short bridges and tunnels. I plan to purchase one of these before my next New England adventure.

So far, I've only had to turn around twice, and both times I was in Vermont seeking out covered bridges, so it was my own fault. At least I had a picture-worthy place to turn around.

\*\*\*

Sometimes the GPS acts as harebrained as a toddler on sugar. In 2019, I was heading home from a writing retreat in New Hampshire and had time for one more adventure along the way. I programmed the address of the Leonard Harrison State Park into the GPS and pulled out of my Walmart parking space before dawn. The road to the park, also known as

Pennsylvania's Grand Canyon, pushed my van to its limit. A narrow, winding lane bordered by deep ditches, punctuated by switchbacks, with steep ascents and descents on loose gravel. I piloted the Vansion slowly and steadily, coffee sloshing in my cup while I gripped the wheel with both hands.

I held the motorhome at ten miles per hour as the tires skidded on the small stones. My focus narrowed to include only the next few feet of road as I painstakingly maneuvered around yet another sharp turn, hoping I wouldn't meet anyone traveling in the opposite direction.

The parking lot was empty when I arrived, two and a half hours before the visitors' center was scheduled to open. I gulped the rest of my coffee and studied the sign near the entrance. It warned of the treacherous trail conditions and beseeched hikers to don proper footwear before considering the one-mile hike to the canyon floor.

I changed my shoes and grabbed my walking poles and pepper spray, and I was locking my door when two other cars pulled in. Two couples climbed out of the cars and ambled toward the lookout platform that also served as the trailhead. I strode past their huddle, intent on hiking down and back up within an hour (the sign said to plan for two). My vacation was ticking to an end and I was still about sixteen hours from home.

The hike started out easy—the path was wide enough for two people side by side, smooth and free of roots from the thousands of feet that had tamped down the trail over the years. After the first switchback the path narrowed to a one-person width and the gentle slope gave way to a grade steep enough to crush my toes into the front of my shoes. I met the second switchback with a leaping step and pivoted to face the next leg of the trail, my walking poles swinging jauntily from my wrists.

Before the third switchback I noticed a near-vertical shortcut trail branching off down the mountain. Taking it would eliminate the next two hairpin turns. Several dead trees promised to break my fall, should I lose traction, and I pushed the image of a broken ankle (or worse) from my mind. I veered off the official trail and slid down the shortcut chute. Bodies could easily disappear here, I thought. A person could tumble into the river and be swept away, never to be found.

When I returned to the established trail, I heard voices. A mother admonished her son to be careful. They were walking on a muddy patch of trail, his chubby toddler hand clutching her index finger, a scowl of concentration on his face. Her voice competed with the roar of the river, finally close enough to recognize. We greeted each other with a smile and I silently urged myself to relax and enjoy the moment. This was worth taking the time to appreciate.

I breathed in the lush pine and moss scents. The air was still damp from the previous night's rainstorm, and the sun was on the rise with no clouds to obstruct it. It held the promise of a sweltering day and I was grateful to have timed my visit while the air still held the night's chill. I walked on, using the poles to slow my gait, stopping to take pictures of waterfalls and creepy shadows and patterns in the mud. Eventually, my feet touched the canyon floor. I crossed the bridge for a different vantage point and discussed the trail challenges with a pair of bicyclists who'd approached from the rail trail that delivers visitors from a longer, but smoother and gentler, approach.

The ascent back to the Vansion was steeper than it seemed when I'd headed down. My legs grew heavier as I climbed, and I stepped carefully to avoid tripping on roots and rocks. The sun peeked through the trees to encourage me with sparkly winks and I climbed back to the top (without shortcuts) in thirty minutes.

As I drove away, I ignored the GPS when it advised me to turn back onto the treacherous dirt road and instead discovered a paved highway winding through farm country that led me west through rolling hills toward home.

Road Trip Rule # 28:

Winter is road-trip-planning
season.

# Wayside Ahead:
# Winterizing

It's daunting. It's overwhelming. It invokes anxiety, self-doubt, and stress. It even sounds impossible: winterizing. As if there's a way to protect against the brutal effects of our least friendly season.

But winterizing is simpler than it sounds.

The plumbing system is the only thing that requires winterizing. Somehow, you have to drain the water, blow air into the lines, then fill them with RV antifreeze.

I start on the drive home from my last camping trip of the season. When I leave the dump station after emptying my black and gray tanks, I open the low point valve and drain the fresh water as I'm driving, so any residual water will flow out as I'm climbing hills and steering around curves.

Once I arrive home, I unload the van as usual: dirty laundry, food from the fridge, and books I've read on the trip. On the last seasonal trip, I also unload all clean clothes, bedding, cleaning supplies, and food from the cabinets. I usually leave paper products behind and I cram the pillows into cabinets in case a mouse finds his way inside during the winter.

Next, I close the low point valve, open the

pressure valve in the furnace/water heater, shut the water heater off, and open the faucets in the kitchen and bathroom, including the shower and toilet. When the water stops coming out, I hook up the air compressor to the water hook-up at the back of the van and blow air into the lines at 40 psi. After that, I close the faucets, bypass the water heater, and pump three gallons of RV antifreeze into the lines. Some people just blow air through the lines; some just put antifreeze in the lines. I do both, mainly so I can rest easy when the temperature dips to thirty or forty below zero during the winter months.

I turn on each faucet until the antifreeze appears, and I let it run for about thirty seconds to fill the trap below each sink. I flush the toilet a few times, until it's filled with pink liquid, and I run the shower until a sufficient amount of antifreeze has gone down the drain. I also pour an additional two or three cups of antifreeze down each drain. It's cheap insurance.

To make sure there's antifreeze in the black and gray tank valves so they don't freeze and crack, open each one for a second and close it again. It'll trap the antifreeze in there. A few drops falling out on the driveway won't do any harm.

Double-check the furnace, water pump, and water heater have all been shut off. Shut off the propane tank. Disconnect the house battery, if your rig has this feature.

All of this takes about fifteen minutes and newer rigs are easier than the older ones. Consult your owners' manuals for specific instructions or view one of the myriad YouTube video tutorials about winterizing campers. I watched a few of the videos, read the owners' manuals, and made myself a cheat sheet customized to my particular rig before attempting it.

You're ready for winter.

Road Trip Rule # 48:

You're exactly where you're
supposed to be.

MILE
2
5

## House Battery

The house batteries continued to set off the smoke alarm whenever the van sat for more than twenty-four hours. The level of charge the batteries held at a given time could be determined by pressing the button on the monitor panel. There are three lights, and when all three lit up, the battery was fully charged. When the bottom light was the only illumination, the smoke alarm shrieked in torturous intervals.

The batteries grew weaker over the summer. On a road trip with two consecutive nights of dry camping, the smoke alarm rocketed me out of bed at 4 am on the second morning. When I started the van to charge the batteries, the smoke alarm continued to shriek for twelve interminable minutes. This seemed rather slow —as if the engine was only providing a trickle charge.

I called the dealership each time the smoke alarm went off but they offered no helpful suggestions or recommendations.

At some point, I realized that the monitor panel lights also indicate when the batteries are receiving a charge. When the van was plugged into shore power, the battery level indicator was fully lit. If I pulled the plug after a few moments, the panel reverted to the true level of charge—one or two lights.

*If it lights up while it's plugged in*, I thought, *it should light up when the engine is running.* I started the van and pressed the battery level button—the bottom light was the only bright spot on the panel. I called the dealership again.

Lucy answered on the first ring. "Is your battery disconnect switch on?"

"The batteries are connected. The lights are working. It's a problem with charging the battery from the engine, while driving."

Lucy promised she'd talk to a technician and call me back. The technician, when he called, had no suggestions that I hadn't already tried, and by then it was time for me to winterize the van and store it for the winter.

The following spring, I called the dealership again and reminded them of my problem.

"I'm driving to Missouri again—if I stop in, will you take a look at it?"

"Yes, we'll take care of you."

I made an appointment and arrived the following week. Within minutes, they determined a fifty-amp fuse, located under the floor between the two front seats, had blown. That fuse protected the line that charged the house batteries.

"We found the problem," said Steve, the technician who'd replaced the fuse.

"That isn't the cause, that's the effect," I said. "What caused the fuse to blow?"

He shook his head. "We'll never know that. We replaced your fuse—you can keep this old one, if you'd like—and Lucy can process your payment."

"Payment? I've had this problem since I bought the van. I've called Lucy several times throughout the year about this."

Steve looked like he wanted to crawl under the nearest RV and stay there until sundown. "Lucy needs to see you."

She handed me a bill for $130.

"Isn't this covered? I've called you about this several times."

Lucy shrugged. "It might've been covered if you'd returned here within a year, but it's been a year and a week since you bought your RV."

"Can I at least have a price break? I spent over sixty thousand dollars here."

She tapped her pen on the counter and sighed. "Our minimum service fee is a hundred dollars. The fuse was thirty. There's nothing I can do about it."

I could feel my entire body getting warmer. My face reddened. "Is it covered under that ridiculously expensive service contract I purchased?"

"No, that's for things in the house part of the rig —not the van."

"Wow." I pulled out my credit card and tossed it on the counter. "I guess when you're this close to Chicago your customer base is so large you don't worry about loyalty."

"Actually, many of our customers return when they're ready to upgrade." She slid my card back to me with the receipt.

"That's good. You won't miss me, then." I turned and walked out the door.

I shook off my anger and disappointment as I climbed into the driver's seat. This whole experience supported my initial inclination to stay nearby on the night I purchased the rig, which I hadn't done. Just another lesson on the costs of impetuous behavior. At least it had been an affordable lesson—it could have been much worse.

The batteries, of course, were weakened by their constant draining. I replaced them the following spring.

# Wayside Ahead:
# Battery Replacement

My current rig has two house batteries located in a bin next to the entry door. They're marine-style, which seems to indicate they're more expensive, heavier, and last longer than regular car batteries.

When I pulled the Jan Van out of storage in the spring, I did what I always do: plugged it into shore power and cleaned it from top to bottom. When the batteries were fully charged I unplugged from shore power while I restocked the cabinets, made the bed, and filled the water tank. A few hours later, the smoke alarm heralded the batteries' failure to hold a charge for even one afternoon.

At first glance, the battery compartment appears packed with batteries and wires. The batteries are connected to the vehicle battery, to the panel in the rear of the van (and subsequently, the generator and power inverter), and to each other. The compartment itself is a metal box with a narrow two inches of space around the batteries. The compartment door is hinged at the top and has no latch to hold it open, and tends to bruise hands or arms when it slams down.

It seems an impossible task to disconnect the wires, maneuver the fifty-pound blocks out, slide the new ones in, and reconnect the wires, all while battling the floppy door and being careful not touch both posts simultaneously with a metal wrench.

Things to consider regarding battery replacement:

- Take a photo of the tops of the batteries, showing the wire placement
- Draw a simple schematic showing all wire connections
- Label each end of each wire with its battery connection (for example, if a wire is attached to the positive terminal on the left battery, it would be labeled L+)
- Watch a few YouTube video tutorials from different RV channels until you're comfortable with the order of operations
- File your schematic sketch in the owner's manual

I spent about two hours planning the battery replacement and fifteen minutes performing it. Next time, I won't be so tentative.

# ROAD WORK ENDS

Road Trip Rule # 117:

Life is a Grand Adventure.

# Grand Adventures

Traveling solo has become my favorite way to see the sights, but I don't always camp alone. Sometimes I camp with a group I met through Jason when we first moved in together. "I can't wait for you to meet the Browns," he'd said. "They're the best people I know. They're like family."

Jason hasn't gone camping since we sold our last pull-behind. At first I felt unbalanced without him, surrounded by his friends at the campgrounds we'd visited so many times together. The first two years after our separation his absence felt like a presence, an invisible friend clinging to my arm. Eventually, I let myself make new camping memories without him.

The Browns camp en masse with a group of friends. They usually stick close to home, camping for a few days or an entire week at a Michigan State Campground within a couple of hours' drive. Many times, I'm included in the camping group message initiated by Angie Brown, where we alert each other about everything from which campsite we've reserved to what each of us will contribute to the menu.

They have elevated the act of camping to a fine art. Within moments of arriving at the campground, they establish a pop-up village by positioning their pull-behind trailers and fifth wheels with the entry doors facing a common area with space for screened tents and portable hammocks and lawn games. Gary Brown helps me select the best spot to park the Vansion. They plug in ice makers and popcorn machines and set up propane grills and gravity chairs. They bring fishing boats and kayaks and inflatable beach toys; they spend days lying on the sand and finding interesting rocks and hiking the campground trails. The kids hang with the grownups or do their own thing. They play games, read books, or go swimming.

Days quickly assume the camp rhythm: the slow beat of relaxation. Annie Brown and I walk together each morning. We tour the campground, then take a path through the woods or meander down the beach or around the neighborhood. Sometimes Angie's husband Lance and their friend Ira prepare a large breakfast; sometimes everyone orders doughnuts and the kids make a doughnut run. Lunches are usually grabbed on the way to the afternoon's adventure, which might be boating, shopping, beach combing, sunbathing, or reading. There's no wrong way to spend the day at the campground.

Sometime in the late afternoon, everyone straggles back to the campers and prepares their part of dinner. There's a different menu theme each evening—sometimes we have a burger bar (veggie burger for me) with every topping imaginable; sometimes it's a taco bar or a grilled cheese bonanza. We each contribute different toppings, condiments, side dishes, and desserts. No camping trip is complete without Annie's Scotcharoos, an irresistible peanut butter-chocolate-butterscotch dessert.

Evenings find us circled around a perfectly symmetrical and robust bonfire built and maintained by Lance, with s'mores, cocktails, and sometimes live music. If we're camping near Lake Superior, Angie and Rachel, Ira's wife, might search for Yooperlites—rocks that glow in the dark—known as sodalite in the rest of the world.

It was during a week-long stay at the Aloha State Campground near Cheboygan, Michigan, that I asked Lauryn, Angie's daughter, to illustrate this book. I'd spent most of each day laboring over the feedback I'd received from my editor. When the Browns headed to the beach after breakfast, I stationed myself at the picnic table beneath my camper awning and focused on the manuscript. (I prefer to be water-adjacent rather than in the water, and working outside with a water view didn't feel much like work.) When I needed a break one afternoon, I wandered over to chat with everyone as they returned from the beach. I saw Lauryn sketching a campfire scene. She told me about her clothing line in a local boutique—t-shirts and tank tops and sweatshirts featuring her art. The drawings perfectly captured the feeling I was trying to evoke with words: calm, ease, peace, and adventure. When I asked her if she'd conjure some similar scenes for me, she said yes.

Camping with the Browns is so different from the camping I do on a solo road trip, it's hard to believe there isn't a different term for it. When I camp alone, I tend to unpack the fewest necessary items at the campsite to save time on set-up and tear-down. If I'm on a road trip I'll stay at a different campground each night and it's not worth the bother of creating a homey atmosphere near the fire ring. If I stick around for a few nights in one place like I did on PEI, I take the van sightseeing during the days, and I don't want to leave things set up while I'm gone from the campsite. And on the nights spent in store parking lots, of course, I don't even leave the vehicle.

When I join friends for a few days, setting up doesn't feel as onerous as it does when I'm alone. I'll unroll my outdoor rug and extend the awning and leave the coffee maker on the counter. I'll leave a chair or two outside and remove the bike from its rack and pedal around the campground or explore some nearby trails, and leave it parked near the door. Sometimes I bring a pot of flowers to brighten up my picnic table. The Vansion feels more like a second home and less like a rolling crash pad with a refrigerator on these languorous holidays. And when I'm lucky enough to find a campsite within or close to the Browns' pop-up village, I don't bother to lock my door.

When I bought the original Jan Van, the road map of my life expanded. The horizon line stopped crowding me and slid back to its original position far, far ahead. Driving the back roads of America I sometimes felt as if only a moment or two had passed since we'd guided the Rolls K'Nardly across the country, before marriage and children and life in general temporarily canceled my travel itineraries. It turned out my life hadn't derailed completely and I simply had to take a hard left and drive through the construction zone until I returned to smooth pavement. Instead of crisscrossing the country with my husband at my side, I discovered I quite like rambling around on my own.

Looking back, I first thought my Grand Adventure was the impulsive trip to Florida. Then I thought my Grand Adventure was my trip to PEI. Now I realize the Grand Adventure is the whole thing—the muumuu lady, my day with Dad, the Minnesota creeper; the generator issues, the GPS misdirections, the rush hours in unfamiliar cities; and the Segway tour, the waterfall hikes, and the bike trails. And, of course, visiting friends along the way and living in a pop-up village with the Browns.

I'm fueled by curiosity. When I look ahead now, there are many possible Point B destinations and I'm eager to see them all. I'll never run out of Grand Adventures.

Traveling solo has changed me for the better: I'm less frantic and more relaxed and purposeful. More content and confident. I'm glad I bought the Jan Van when I did, and I'm thankful for the canceled plans, route changes, and mechanical maladies, all of which helped me realize I can handle just about anything.

My advice? If you have a burning desire to travel or look up an old friend or learn a foreign language, don't wait. Do something to move closer to your goal today. You never know what's around the bend.

I learned this long ago from the sign on my friend's wall.

Enjoy yourself. It's later than you think.

# Appendix

# GLOSSARY

**Boondocking**: Camping or parking overnight with no hook-ups, as if you're in the boondocks.

**Camper**: One who camps, or a structure in which people camp. Includes pop-ups, pull-behinds, and fifth wheels.

**Class A Motorhome**: The largest style of drivable RV, with the appearance of a bus, usually built on a sturdy steel bus-type chassis. Class A Motorhomes have a box-like appearance with large front windows, and some offer a driver's door and 'house' door, but no passenger door.

**Class B Motorhome**: The smallest style of drivable RV, with the appearance of a van. Conversion vans, camper vans, and any van outfitted for prolonged travel fall into this category. There's a subset of Class B referred to as Class B+, which occupies the thin space between a true B and a C. Class B+ motorhomes are built on a van chassis with the area behind the cab of the original van replaced with a larger, boxier 'house'. There is no sleeping area above the cab in a Class B+.

**Class C Motorhome**: These RVs feature a van chassis with an added house, and the main distinctive commonality of an overcab sleeping area. This overcab bed allows for more living space without increasing the square footage of the cabin floor.

**Conversion Van**: See Class B Motorhome definition.

**Converter**: A device that converts 110 volts to 12 volts. In an RV, a converter automatically engages when you're plugged into shore power. Many RV lights and appliances run on a 12-volt system; the converter ensures these components don't burn up from high voltage.

**Diesel Pusher**: A type of Class A Motorhome that features a disel engine located near the rear of the vehicle.

**Digital Nomad:** Person who lives in their RV full-time and makes money using their computer and a WiFi signal. They might work for themselves or for a company.

**Dry Bathroom**: A bathroom that features a shower unit that closes off from the rest of the bathroom, so the bathroom itself remains dry. (See also: Wet Bathroom)

**Dry Camping:** camping with no hook-ups.

**Full-Timer:** Person who lives in their RV full-time and doesn't own a house at a fixed address. (See also:

Part-Timer)

**Inverter**: A device that converts 12 volts to 110 volts. In an RV, an inverter is usually operated by engaging a switch. It's used when you're not connected to shore power and you don't have your generator running, but you want to plug something into a regular 110-volt outlet. Familiarize yourself with your individual RV's electrical system before using the inverter.

**Part-Timer**: Person who lives part of the time in their RV, and part of the time in their own fixed-address house or with friends or relatives. (See also: Full-Timer)

**Pop-Up**: A small trailer that features either a manual crank or a motorized mechanism that lifts the roof to expose canvas walls and slide-out beds. A pop-up is half hard trailer and half tent and usually has a small refrigerator and stove. Some also have a microwave and a toilet with a zipper door, and most of them have a dinette. The advantages of a pop-up include maneuverability and cost, while the disadvantages are lack of space and amenities.

**Pull-Behind**: Also called a hard-sided trailer. A trailer with solid walls that connects to a vehicle for towing. Pull-behinds are the most popular of all RV types, and they come in a vast array of styles and sizes from thirteen to forty feet long. These trailers act as second homes for those who travel for extended periods, or as semi-permanent dwellings on vacant land or season-long stays at campsites. Some fairly standard features include sturdy doors that lock, air conditioning, a dry bathroom, and plenty of storage niches. Many have slide-outs to increase floor space and livability.

**Reflectix**: brand name of insulating product. It's lightweight, reasonably priced, and silver, so it reflects the heat. Available in many stores, including Amazon.com.

**RV**: Recreational Vehicle. Specifically, a vehicle in which people camp. Includes pop-ups, pull-behinds, fifth wheels, conversion vans, Class A motorhomes, Class B motorhomes, and Class C motorhomes.

**Shore Power:** an outlet "on land". Preferably, an outlet of the proper amperage for your rig. Most small and older RVs require a 30-amp outlet. The newer and larger RVs require a 50-amp outlet. Standard outlets, such as those on the outside of a house or garage, are usually on a 20-amp circuit. You can purchase an adapter to make your plug fit into the 20-amp outlet, but you'll cause the breaker to trip if you use more than one or two electrical items at a time. If you have a voltage monitor installed, watch the readout to determine how to balance your load.

**Slide-Out**: Portion of RV that extends outward to expand the living area. Slide-outs are kept stowed during transportation, and extended while securely parked on a level surface. They are usually designed to expand the kitchen/living room area, but some slide the bed out to make it easier to walk around it.

**Tiny Home:** A house designed for full-time living,

usually built on a trailer so it can be relocated, although most tiny homes aren't used for road trips or short camping trips. A tiny home is generally less than 900 square feet, customized to the owners' preferences, and built with house-quality construction techniques. It's a perfect blend of mobile home portability and custom carpentry.

**Voltage Monitor:** A device that constantly measures the voltage. This is very helpful if you're wondering if a campground or other source of shore power is providing adequate voltage, and it can help you decide which electric items to operate simultaneously and balance your electrical load so you don't experience low voltage, which can harm appliances.

**Wet Bathroom**: A bathroom that features a shower head on the wall—the drain is in the floor, possibly beneath a removable panel. There is generally very little storage in a wet bathroom, as everything must be removed during a shower. This type of shower saves space in the overall floor plan, but for me, its inconvenience outweighs its utility. (See also: Dry Bathroom)

# RESOURCES

**Smartphone Apps:**

Airbnb (for classes and other experiences)

Campendium (for campground locations, reviews, and contact information, as well as public land and free camping sites and dump station locations)

Overnight RV Parking (for a comprehensive list of free RV parking locations, including WalMart and other stores)

Park Advisor (for campground locations, reviews, and contact information)

RV Life (campground locations and information, trip routing software, RV-related articles)

RV Parky (RV park locations, reviews, and contact information)

**Books:**

*RV Capital of the World: A Fun-Filled Indiana History* by Al Hesselbart

*RVs & Campers 1900 - 2000: An Illustrated History* by Donald F. Wood

*RV Electricity* by Mike Sokol

Washington Post Article:
https://www.washingtonpost.com/business/2018/11/12/million-americans-live-rvs-meet-modern-nomads/

*Work From Home While You Roam: The Ultimate Guide to Jobs That Can Be Done From Anywhere* by Robin Barrett


**Websites:**

Anne of Green Gables Provincial Park:
www.pc.gc.ca

Forest River Owners' Group (FROG):
www.forestriverfrog.com/

Grandfather Mountain:
www.ncparks.gov/grandfather-mountain-state-park/home

The Mack Theatre in Charlottetown, PEI:
    www.confederationcentre.com/venues/the-mack/

Missouri Star Quilt Company in Hamilton, MO:
    www.missouriquiltco.com/

Pennsylvania's Grand Canyon:
    www.pacanyon.com/

RVElectricity.com

RV/MH Hall of Fame:
    www.rvmhhalloffame.org

RVTravel.com

Ryder Carroll's YouTube video about Bullet Journals:
    https://bit.ly/YouTubeBuJo

Segway Tours in Summerside, PEI:
    www.peisegway.com

The Wild Center near Tupper Lake, NY:
    www.wildcenter.org

Yarn Junction near Des Moines, IA:
    www.yarnjunction.com

## ACKNOWLEDGEMENTS

Writing this book was much like taking a spontaneous road trip. I had no preplanned route, no itinerary, and I didn't know which luggage to bring or what to put in it.

Quite a few friends suggested I write about my solo travels, and I finally decided to do so after completing an assignment at the Birth a Book writing retreat led by Dorothy Holtermann in Bethlehem, New Hampshire. At first, the subject sat uneasily with me. Many of the personal experiences included in this book were difficult to write about, and I wasn't sure I wanted to expose them to the light of day. On the other hand, those same experiences pushed me to fast-track my road trip dreams and buy that first Jan Van. Dorothy encouraged me to "go deep" and "tell the whole story".

A few months after the retreat, something broke loose. Perhaps my muse awoke; perhaps I was finally comfortable writing about the past; perhaps the long, dark UP winter infused me with writing energy. Whatever the reason, I finished the first draft in a blizzard of inspiration and activity.

This book, like all books, is a solitary project that owes its life to collaboration. It could not have been completed without my team of beta readers and developmental editors. Thank you to my sister Jen Postula, my friend and editor Kelly Cox, friend and beta reader Megan Atkinson, and my friend, writing partner, and developmental editor Sara Maurer for encouraging me to finish this book. Aunt Karen Bryant read an early manuscript and provided vital information about the Australia years. And I truly appreciate Angie Leonard's willingness to perform an eleventh-hour perusal with pencil in hand. I owe each of you a dinner out, a bottle of wine, and a copy of the book.

Thank you to Lauryn Brown for the fabulous illustrations. Lauryn's rendition of the Rolls K'Nardly brings back many fan belt moments.

The RV/MH Hall of Fame is worth a stop, if you're even remotely interested in camping. Their display of campers includes many of the models I mentioned in the book, arranged along an indoor walking path with an informational plaque near each one. After touring the campers (twice), I chatted with Anna at the front desk. She advised me to visit the RV resource library located on the second floor of the Hall of Fame—a quiet room lined with thousands of copies of RV lifestyle magazines, owners' manuals, and RV industry periodicals. In other words, a treasure trove! I gleaned most of my historical information from articles found in the library.

Last, but far from least, thank you to the friends who include me in their camping plans or offer a Vansion-sized parking spot whenever I glide in for a visit.

# Other Books by Jan Stafford Kellis

### *Bookworms Anonymous: A Non-Traditional Book Club for All Readers*

Part memoir, part cookbook, and part informational guide, this is an exclusive peek inside the closed society of Bookworms Anonymous, a non-traditional book club in De Tour Village, located in Michigan's Upper Peninsula. This book takes the reader to eight book club meetings (they're *never* called parties) and includes book reviews, book handling commandments, recipes, and a guide for beginning your own chapter of Bookworms Anonymous.

### *Bookworms Anonymous: Volume II*

The women are gathered again! Bookworms Anonymous is a non-traditional reading group established in 2000, comprised of seven women in

Michigan's Upper Peninsula. They meet monthly to share a gourmet vegetarian meal and discuss and swap books. Part memoir, part cookbook and part celebration of words and reading, Bookworms Anonymous Volume II contains many of the same things found in Volume I: reading group meetings, anecdotes, book reviews and recipes.

"A delightful read for any book lover, Bookworms Anonymous II is packed with great reading recommendations and insightful conversation from seven savvy readers. Book club-friendly recipes are a delicious bonus! Now, I'm off to the bookstore..."
- Kathleen Flinn, author of *The Sharper Your Knife, the Less You Cry* and *The Kitchen Counter Cooking School*

"A warm celebration of two of life's most vital ingredients--books and friendships."
- Ellen Airgood, author of *South of Superior* and *Prairie Evers*

"A love letter to reading, beautifully rendered, and with all the warmth and fun and closeness of your favorite book club on that perfect meeting night."
- Robert Kurson, author of *Shadow Divers* and *Crashing Through*

## The Word That You Heard

Enid Forrester hates her name and her hair. On the first day of summer in 1980 she can almost see the wonderfully empty expanse of time stretching before her. Enid comes of age in Michigan's Upper Peninsula, where there isn't much to do in the summer or any other time of year for a twelve-year-old girl. Her summer education includes listening to the "drunken pontificators" lecture in the coffee shop about what not to do as she joins her dad at the local table for their morning refueling. Enid learns life can't be distilled into mere words and small towns sometimes offer the widest view of humanity.

## A Pocketful of Light

Italy has it all and she's willing to share. Explore the world's original tourist destination through this true story told like a novel. The book features the Fibonacci Sequence, a few non-painful history lessons and some funky Italian phrases as well as the friendly recounting of two travelers exploring the second greatest country in the world.

## Superior Sacrifices

A tale of betrayal, redemption and the consequences of silence by the author of Bookworms Anonymous and The Sunshine Room. This is the story of Mitch and Marcia: twins, best friends and local celebrities in the small town of Iron Falls, Michigan. Mitch's superhuman dedication to his detective job and Marcia's near-obsessive focus on her family and bookstore business appear ordinary until the secret they've shared for three and a half decades threatens to surface.

## The Sunshine Room

Ellen and her daughter Althea share an apartment in Chicago. A Universe of two, they live a simple life and take care of each other. When Ellen receives a call urging her to her estranged father's hospital bedside, Ellen wonders whether or not she should respond.

Is Ellen ready to face her own past, and subject Althea to the long-held secrets she left behind?

Will Althea embark on her own journey to discover the past she didn't know she had?

All books are available in fine book stores and online.

## About The Author

Jan Stafford Kellis lives in the wild woods of Michigan's Upper Peninsula where she operates her one-woman micro business, the DeTour Soap Company. She reads and writes every day, and frequently finds time to make soap, go glamping, knit, crochet, quilt, make paper flowers or spray glitter on something. She's a marathon shopper and loves to hang out with her sister and visit her daughters and granddaughters. Jan is a founding member of the writing group *Inklings*, a charter member of the reading group *Bookworms Anonymous*, and a founding member of the *JAM Book Club and Biker Gang*.

To catch up on the latest news or book an appearance, please visit jankellis.com.

CPSIA information can be obtained
at www.ICGtesting.com
Printed in the USA
FSHW022342230621
82592FS